FIND THE LADY

FIND THE LADY

by Michael Pertwee

JOSEF WEINBERGER PLAYS

LONDON

FIND THE LADY
First published in 1979
by Josef Weinberger Ltd
(pka English Theatre Guild Ltd/Warner/Chappell Plays Ltd)
12-14 Mortimer Street, London, W1T 3JJ

This edition first published 2003

ISBN 0 85676 043 9

Printed by Wrightsons, Earls Barton, Northants, England.

Find the Lady was first presented at the Alexandra Theatre, Birmingham on 28 May 1979, with the following cast:

MRS PRATT	Margaret Inglis
DESIREE PRATT	Patsy Rowlands
DOCTOR ALI	John Eastham
ROSIE LAKE	Mollie Sugden
MARK ANDERSON	Richard Latham
TIM CANTEL	Bill Pertwee
MISS DAINTEE	Rosamunde Hartley
JEAN SMITH	Kirsten Cooke

Directed by Wallace Douglas

Author's note:

FIND THE LADY is a comedy-thriller and, as such, is a hybrid which is described in the Oxford Dictionary as, "A thing composed of incongruous elements". It is a challenging type of play and care has to be taken to insure that the comedy does not kill the thrills and the thrills do not stifle the comedy.

The secret of a successful production of this kind of play is pace. The audience should be given time to laugh but not much else. The action should move so fast that no one has the opportunity to probe too deeply into motivation, red-herrings and comedy-thrill situations. This is not to say that is should be played farcically. If the aim is to thrill as well as to amuse then the characters must be believable human beings, so the temptation to overplay should be firmly resisted. This is particularly true of the character of ROSIE LAKE, the leading role. Hopefully she will be very funny but she must emerge as a believable, lovable character and not a caricature.

CAST OF CHARACTERS

THE LADY *

ROSIE LAKE

MRS PRATT

TIM CANTEL

MISS DAINTEE **

MARK ANDERSON

DESIREE PRATT

DOCTOR ALI

JEAN SMITH

Note:

* THE LADY speaks only a few lines and makes one brief appearance
** MISS DAINTEE appears throughout the play but is a non-speaking role.

Synopsis of scenes

The action of the play takes place in the lounge of the Delamere Private Hotel, South Kensington, London SW7 3LG.

Time: The Present

ACT ONE

Scene One: Monday 2.00 am.
Scene Two: Monday 12.30 pm.

ACT TWO

Monday 8.30 pm.

ACT ONE

Scene One

The Lounge of the Delamere Private Hotel, London.
Time: Monday 2.00 am.

A Victorian room, shabbily furnished, with an air of faded
grandeur. UR at an angle and separating the back wall from
the R wall is a door marked DINING ROOM. In the centre of
the back wall is an alcove with an aperture of some six feet
and a depth of some four feet. In it are two chairs, one against
either wall. Also a card table, folded flat and leaning against
back wall. There are curtains to this alcove, which can be
drawn to cut it from view. (Note: for reasons which will
become evident there must be a well-disguised secret exit from
this alcove, enabling an actor to exit unseen once the curtains
are closed.)

UL at an angle and separating the back wall from the L wall
is a door which (presumably) leads to hall and front door. In
the L wall is a bay window with a padded seat. This window
can be cut off by curtains which are drawn straight across,
thus concealing the whole bay area. On the R wall is a
fireplace and bookshelves. There are two small, low chairs
against the R wall, one above the fireplace and one below it.

DSR is a sofa, Behind the sofa is a table on which are assorted
magazines. DSC is a smallish tub armchair. DSL is a
high-backed armchair beside which is an occasional table.
UL on the wall above window bay is a sideboard, on which is
a whisky bottle and some glasses. DL on wall below window
bay is a desk, with a stool. On the back wall to L of alcove is
a table on which is a telephone. On the wall above there is
also a key rack with various keys on it. There are light
switches at door UR, door UL and just outside the alcove.

The stage is in darkness, except for a dim glow from the dying
embers of a fire and perhaps a little filtered moonlight
through a crack in the drawn curtains over the bay window.
The curtains of the alcove are also closed. The UL door to hall
is open. The UR door to dining room is closed.

Fairly distantly is heard the sound of two cats miaowing.

A light in the hall seen through door UL comes on and THE
LADY'S *voice is heard.*

THE LADY   (*offstage*) No! Leave me alone! Have you lost
                    your mind? Aaah!

                    (THE LADY *enters from hall. She runs into the
                    room, slams the door, switches on the lights
                    and locks the door with shaky hand. She is
                    middle-aged, quite well dressed and made up
                    in a way which indicates a desire to look
                    younger than she is. She wears a top coat and
                    carries quite a large handbag. She is
                    breathless and scared and somewhat
                    dishevelled. Someone outside the door pushes
                    against it and rattles the handle.*)

                    Go away! Do you hear me? I'll say nothing if
                    you leave me in peace. Are you there? (*Silence
                    from outside door.*) You'll only make things
                    worse for yourself. Answer me! Are you there?
                    I know you're there. (*Still silence from outside
                    door.*) Very well. I shall call the police and tell
                    them everything.

                    (*Still no sign of an answer.* THE LADY *now
                    moves to the telephone and, still looking
                    towards the door UL, dials 999. A click from
                    dining room door UR makes her wheel round.
                    A gloved hand comes into view.* THE LADY
                    *gives a gasp of terror drops the receiver,
                    which hangs down, swinging. The gloved hand
                    switches off the lights by the door UR. As the
                    stage is plunged into darkness* THE LADY
                    *utters a muted scream. NB: The audience will
                    see nothing more than two vague shadows,
                    one of which moves swiftly from R to L. The
                    shadows meet and move towards alcove,
                    locked together.* THE LADY *utters a strangled
                    choking sound which is gradually silenced
                    and eventually drowned by the miaows, nearer
                    this time, of the two cats. A shadow moves L.*

Sound of lock turning and then the door to hall opens a trifle, only a matter of an inch or so. A little light is seen. Rosie's *voice is heard offstage.*

Rosie   (*offstage*) Raggles! Where are you? Puss! Puss! Puss!

(The hall door closes audibly. The shadow swiftly moves back R. Sound of exertion and something being dragged along the floor. Door UL opens again. Rosie Lake *enters and switches on the lights by door to hall. She is the proprietress of the hotel, an ex-actress who lets you know this. She is very short-sighted, extremely vague and is apt to hit the bottle, ostensibly only at weekends. She often carries a large fan. She generally affects gaudy-looking spectacles but, on this occasion, does not wear any. She is clothed in a flowing dressing-gown and nightdress and has her hair in huge curlers under a scarf. NB: For the purposes of quick changing these curlers can be attached to the inside of the scarf and not actually to her hair, except perhaps for a couple at the front.* The Lady *lies face down on the floor with most of her body outside the alcove. Only her feet and a small part of her legs are inside, hidden by the curtains, which are moving slightly. Her head is turned towards the R.)*

Rosie   Raggles! Puss! Puss!

*(*Rosie's *myopia is immediately established as she moves carefully into the room and starts to feel around the sideboard for her glasses.)*

Oh, where are those blessed glasses?

*(*Rosie *clicks her teeth angrily then moves R and walks right past, and almost over, the prostrate body of* The Lady *without noticing anything.)*

Puss! Puss!

(ROSIE *goes to dining room door and looks
through.*)

Pussy!

(ROSIE *turns back and, once again, walks right
past the body of* THE LADY, *again without any
reaction.*)

Sometimes I could strangle you!

(ROSIE *goes to sideboard, picks up the whisky
bottle and prepares to open the screw top.* THE
LADY'S *body makes a tiny, silent movement as
somebody unseen evidently pulls at her feet to
drag her into alcove.* ROSIE *suddenly freezes in
a very late delayed reaction. She slowly turns
and looks back at the body.*)

Oh! Who's that? Miss Daintee?

(ROSIE *moves to front of alcove and looks
down at* THE LADY. *She carries the bottle.*)

ROSIE   Mrs Privett-Thing? What are you doing down
there? Get up! Oh, no!

(ROSIE *steps over the body so that her feet are
either side of it and her back is to alcove
against the curtains.*)

Mrs Privett-Smith! Are you . . . ?

(ROSIE *suddenly freezes because of something
she has heard or perhaps felt through the
curtains of the alcove. She half turns.*)

Who's there?

(*As* ROSIE *starts to part the curtains a gloved
hand simultaneously comes out of the side of
the curtain near telephone and turns off the*

lights. Rosie *utters a loud yell. There is the sound of a thump of something hitting something. A gasp from* Rosie *then the thud of a body falling. Again we are in almost complete darkness; but we may detect one figure dragging another figure towards the R*. [*Alternatively, at Director's discretion, we can cheat here and have* The Lady *slip into alcove and she and the mystery assailant will leave quietly by the secret exit. This may be better for the subsequent scene between* Rosie *and* Mrs Pratt, *when we may think that both body of* The Lady *and the figure of assailant are still there behind the curtains.] Distantly a woman's voice is heard calling.*)

Mrs Pratt   (*distantly offstage*) What is happening? Miss Lake?

(*A groan is heard from* Rosie. *Hall door opens wide and the figure of* Mrs Pratt *is seen silhouetted in the doorway, with walking cane raised in a defensive/aggressive position.* Rosie *groans again.*)

Is someone there?

(Mrs Pratt *switches on the lights at door. She is elderly, sharp-tongued and all there. She invariably walks with the aid of her cane.* Rosie *lies on the floor outside alcove, the curtains of which are closed. The whisky bottle lies beside her. The receiver of phone dangles from the instrument. Of* The Lady's *body there is no sign.*)

This is intolerable . . .

(Rosie *dizzily staggers to her feet, lurches towards* Mrs Pratt *and flings her arms round her in a near hysterical state.*)

Rosie   Don't look, Mrs Potter! Don't look!

MRS PRATT	(*fighting free*) Don't look at what?
ROSIE	(*a backward wave*) The body.
MRS PRATT	(*looking*) What body?
ROSIE	That body! Mrs Privett-Smith I think. Dead. Murdered.
MRS PRATT	What nonsense is this? There's nobody there.

(ROSIE *turns, stares, peers myopically at the spot and reacts. She sways dizzily and puts a hand to the top of her head.*)

ROSIE	There is. Was. Lying there. Dead. And a man smashed me on the head. Would have killed me but for me curlers . . .
MRS PRATT	Tchah!

(MRS PRATT *pushes* ROSIE *aside and walks towards alcove. She stretches out a hand to the curtains.*)

ROSIE	(*a yell*) No! Careful! Still there!

(MRS PRATT, *ignoring this, throws open the curtains to reveal the alcove empty except for the two chairs and a card table folded up and leaning against back wall.* ROSIE *staggers R and stares into the alcove. That's impossible! Saw her. He hit me.* MRS PRATT *picks up the whisky bottle which she hands to* ROSIE, *who takes it.*)

MRS PRATT	This is what hit you, Miss Lake. You were intoxicated before going to bed and are still more so now.
ROSIE	(*outraged*) Oooooh! Do you think I'd imagine –
MRS PRATT	Yes!
ROSIE	I saw Mrs Privett-Smith lying. (*Makes awful face.*) With her eyes bulging and her tongue –

MRS PRATT	Mrs Privett-Smith went away for the weekend. Her room is empty. I looked in on the way down. Go to bed and sleep it off. Much more of this and I shall move to an hotel where the proprietor does not get drunk and disorderly.
ROSIE	With my own eyes I saw her . . .
MRS PRATT	It'll be pink elephants next.

(MRS PRATT *exits into hall.* ROSIE *rubs her head and winces. She moves to sideboard, starts to open bottle to give herself a drink, then changes her mind. She shakes her head, looking very worried. We can almost read her thoughts. Did she imagine it? She turns away, turns back and picks up the bottle. This time she holds it as a weapon as she crosses from L to R and exits into dining room, cautiously, on tiptoe. Offstage sound of front door closing. Offstage sound of something being dragged along the floor.* TIM CANTEL *(the Squadron Leader) enters backwards through the open door from hall. He is pulling a large old cabin trunk. He could wear a topcoat or raincoat. He is a handsome man in a slightly raffish way. His age is uncertain but he is neither a kid nor a Battle of Britain veteran. He hums to himself, dragging the trunk after him. He backs into the alcove and starts to pull trunk in after him.* ROSIE, *with bottle, enters from dining room. She sees the trunk sliding, apparently by itself, into the alcove and lets out a shriek, which also startles* CANTEL. CANTEL *hurries out of alcove and looks at* ROSIE, *who has remained rooted to the spot.*)

CANTEL	Rosie! You're up late.
ROSIE	Ah! Oh! It's you, Squadron Leader! What are you doing scaring me like that?
CANTEL	Just shoving this old trunk of mine in here . . .

ROSIE   You shouldn't shove trunks about in the
           middle of the night; could give a person a heart
           attack.

           (ROSIE, *on rubber legs, moves L and goes to
           sideboard where she pours herself a hefty
           drink.* CANTEL *eyes her with a quizzical smile.
           He pushes the trunk right into alcove and also
           replaces the telephone.*)

CANTEL   In a bit of a tizzy, aren't you?

ROSIE   So would you be. Tim, would you say I was
           drunk?

CANTEL   No.

ROSIE   So if I told you that five minutes ago I saw Mrs
           Privett-Smith lying here dead, that someone
           knocked me out and when I came to, a minute
           later, there was the body – gone. What would
           you say to that?

CANTEL   That you were drunk!

ROSIE   So would I and so will everybody.

           (ROSIE *flops into tub chair.* CANTEL *feels in his
           pocket and hangs a front door key on the key
           rack.*)

CANTEL   Anyway, Privett's away, isn't she?

ROSIE   'She' could have come back. She had a key. It's
           not there, is it?

CANTEL   Front door key? No. Only the one I just put
           back. (*Moves down to her.*) Rosie, love, didn't
           you say something about it being your
           birthday?

ROSIE   Tomorrow . . . (*Squints closely at her watch.*)
           Well, today, yes.

CANTEL   (*elbow gesture*) Maybe you were celebrating . . .

ROSIE	NO! You should feel this lump on me head.
CANTEL	I can see half a dozen!
ROSIE	Those are me curlers. But for them I could have been killed myself. It can't have been a hallucy-thing. It can't.
CANTEL	Why not? You've got one corpse upstairs in her coffin, haven't you? Enough to give anyone the heeby-jeebies.
ROSIE	Of course I'm upset about Lucy Fordyce dying but it wasn't that. (*Not sure.*) I'm sure. (*Shudders.*) Her tongue-sticking out. She'd been strangled.
CANTEL	(*gestures to phone*) Want me to call the cops?
ROSIE	(*hesitates*) N-no. They'd only ask where the body's got to.
CANTEL	I was coming round to that myself. If it only happened minutes ago where is the body? Where is the killer?
ROSIE	He could have carried her out into the street.
CANTEL	Slung over his shoulder, out in the open? Anyway, l was out there for some time and I ain't seen nobody.
ROSIE	Well, I don't know. He could have put her in a . . . (*Her eyes go towards alcove.*) t . . .
CANTEL	In a what?
ROSIE	(*embarrassed*) Well – a trunk. Oh! I didn't mean . . .
CANTEL	(*chuckles*) Want to have a look? I'll give you a thousand quid for every stiff you find in that trunk.
ROSIE	I'm sorry. (*Turns to him.*) But what are you doing shoving a great trunk into my alcove?

CANTEL   It's only for a day or so; saves me humping it
            upstairs. (*Glance towards door, lowers voice.*)
            I'm leaving, Rosie. I've packed in my job at the
            flying club. That's all my gear.

ROSIE   Leaving?

CANTEL   Landed a fabulous job abroad.

            (ROSIE'S *mind is obviously wandering back to
            her experience.*)

ROSIE   Oh, that's nice.

            (ROSIE *rises, wanders back towards the table
            and bottle.*)

CANTEL   But don't tell any of the other inmates. For
            personal reasons I want to keep it quiet. Okay?

ROSIE   (*lifting bottle*) H'm?

CANTEL   I said don't tell anyone about my leaving or
            about the new job.

ROSIE   Oh. No. Whatever you say.

CANTEL   (*kisses her cheek*) I'm going to turn in.
            (*Indicates bottle.*) I'd suggest Horlicks rather
            than scotch, less likely to give you more
            nightmares. 'Night.

            (CANTEL *waves and exits into hall. ROSIE
            hesitates about the bottle and finally decides
            against another drink. She puts bottle down,
            moves to door and switches off the lights. She
            is now clearly silhouetted by the light from
            hall. Suddenly and terrifyingly loud comes the
            sound of two cats yelling their heads off. ROSIE
            clutches her heart and nearly fails. Then she
            realises what it is, runs to window and draws
            back the curtains as the cats continue to
            screech. They stop as she flings curtains wide.*)

ROSIE   (*shouting*) Get away! Get off you brute! Leave
                 my pussy alone!

                 (*Blackout.*)

                        Scene Two

Time: Monday 12.30 pm. The lights rise to show daylight
through windows. The fire is out. Alcove curtains are closed.
MISS DAINTEE *enters UL from hall. She is a weird-looking old*
lady with a penchant for beads and a hairstyle which looks as
if she wears earphones. She has a furtive manner. She carries
a large cloth bag. Her eyes dart hither and thither. She comes
DS and stands behind high-backed chair. She sees something
on the floor, bends and picks it up. It is a knife with a curved
blade – a kukri. She stands for a moment with her arm poised
and the knife held aloft. Something on the occasional table
beside the chair catches her eye. She drops the knife on to the
seat of the high-backed chair. She picks up a small silver
ornament from the table and furtively pops it into her bag. She
moves R and pauses by the table behind the sofa where she
picks up another ornament, which she also puts into the bag.
Now she moves back US towards the alcove. She reaches out
and opens one of the curtains. Startlingly, a man is instantly
revealed, scaring her. This is MARK ANDERSON, *a good-looking*
man in his 30s, clad in a shabby sports coat and grey trousers.
He looks a bit sheepish. As MISS DAINTEE *gives a squeak of*
terror MARK *fairly gently grabs her and puts a hand over her*
mouth.

MARK   Sssssh! It's okay, Miss Daintee. Relax!
                 (*Touches her bag and grins.*) Hm! Quite a haul,
                 eh? Don't worry. I didn't see you and you
                 didn't see me. Right?

                 (MARK *releases her and, without replying,*
                 MISS DAINTEE *scuttles away and exits UR*
                 through dining room door. MARK *watches her*
                 go with a little frown. He turns and closes the
                 alcove curtain. It will have been noted that
                 CANTEL'S *trunk is still in the alcove, in the*
                 same position. MARK *turns towards telephone*
                 table and glances up at the key rack on wall.

A man's voice is heard, off. MARK *moves away DS towards table behind sofa and picks up a magazine as* CANTEL *enters from hall. He carries a bottle of champagne and a white card with a string attached to it.)*

MARK   Hi, there, Squadron Leader.

CANTEL   Morning.

            (CANTEL *moves towards him and puts champagne on the table.)*

MARK   You missed breakfast.

CANTEL   Monday. Kedgeree. Always make a point of missing that. Besides, I was late to bed.

MARK   You missed all the fun. The place has been in an uproar.

CANTEL   Had a helping of that last night, thanks. How is Rosie this morning?

MARK   (*gestures*) I think she has more or less decided it was all in her mind.

CANTEL   Thank Gawd for that. (*Pats his jacket.*) Damn! Got a pen on you?

MARK   Sorry, no. (*Indicates champagne.*) Celebrating?

CANTEL   Rosie's birthday.

MARK   (*moving L*) An unwise present today I'd have thought.

            (MARK *waves casually and exits into hall. Searching for a pen,* CANTEL *moves towards desk.* DESIREE PRATT *enters from hail. She is a fading 40; hopeless but ever hopeful. She is that awful thing, 'A Damned Good Sort'.)*

DESIREE   (*joyfully*) Timmy! It *was* your voice. Heard you were back.

CANTEL   (*not overjoyed*) Oh, hello, Desiree. Yes, got in
             late last night.

DESIREE   Super! Nice weekend? Missed you.

             (DESIREE *runs to him, puts her arms out and
             squeezes him towards her. He moves quickly
             back, glancing towards door.*)

CANTEL   Steady, sweetie! Someone might come in.

DESIREE   So what? We're not breaking any laws!

CANTEL   I know, but remember what I said last week . . .

DESIREE   You've been acting very strangely, Timmy, I
             know you're a bit scared of Mummy, but . . .

CANTEL   I'm not a bit scared of Mummy. I'm utterly
             terrified of her.

DESIREE   (*laughs*) Honestly!

CANTEL   Just for the present it's important that nobody
             has any ideas about us so play it cool. You
             know, none of the burning looks and little
             notes. Right?

DESIREE   If you say so, but . . .

CANTEL   I do and if I seem offhand or you catch me
             chatting up some bird it's all part of the act,
             okay?

DESIREE   I'd like to see you finding a bird to chat up in
             this place! Timmy, I wish you'd tell me why all
             the secrecy.

CANTEL   I will. I promise but, for the moment, mum's the
             word, and particularly your mum.

DESIREE   (*nods*) Okay, but I'm very cross with you. You
             could at least have knocked on my door when
             you came back last night.

CANTEL   It was two in the morning. Besides I got
              waylaid by a lovely bird.

DESIREE   What!

CANTEL   In curlers, clutching the whisky bottle and
              giving one of her more dramatic theatrical
              performances.

DESIREE   (*laughs, relieved*) Rosie!

CANTEL   (*nods*) Our proprietress in person. Remember
              the burglar in the linen cupboard who mugged
              her – and it turned out she'd tripped over the
              Hoover? Well, this was worse. Murder, this
              time.

DESIREE   You don't have to tell me! Mumsie had it, too.
              She heard Rosie screaming and came down to
              see what was happening.

CANTEL   (*surprised*) Oh? That must have been before I
              pitched up. Did she see anything?

DESIREE   Of course not! Just Rosie showing her a corpse
              that wasn't there and saying someone had
              coshed her – again! And she was at it at eight
              o'clock this morning.

CANTEL   Eight! What a constitution! I didn't think she'd
              surface before lunch. What was she on about
              now?

DESIREE   Checking to make sure everyone was alive, I
              think! We were!

CANTEL   Mother Privett-Smith returned, then?

DESIREE   No, and until she has, Rosie won't be really
              happy.

CANTEL   Neither will any of us. Never thought I'd look
              forward to greeting the Privett-Smith; but this
              is it.

DESIREE	Seriously, though, I am a bit worried about Rosie. I mean she was even checking in Lucy Fordyce's room.
CANTEL	(*reacts*) She didn't expect to find Lucy Fordyce alive, I hope? She's been in her coffin since Saturday.
DESIREE	Well, I saw Rosie in her room, standing by the coffin and talking to herself.
CANTEL	(*shakes head*) It's going to be another of those days.

(CANTEL *moves back towards the bottle, thus drawing* DESIREE'S *attention to it.*)

Got a pen on you?

DESIREE	'Fraid not. Ooh, champagne!
CANTEL	Little present . . .
DESIREE	(*hopes it's for her*) Ooh!
CANTEL	(*hastily*) For Rosie.
DESIREE	Oh!
CANTEL	(*moving L*) Must find a pen for the card.
DESIREE	(*making the best of it*) That's nice. That will cheer her up (*Moves after him.*) Though perhaps you should keep it until after Lucy Fordyce's coffin's left. Champagne looks a bit, er . . . Oh, that reminds me. I wonder if our sheaf of flowers arrived.

(CANTEL *exits UL and* DESIREE *exits just after him. Dining room door opens and* MISS DAINTEE *pops her head out. Seeing room is empty she enters. She moves L and passes the table with the champagne bottle on it. She picks up the bottle of champagne. She moves towards hall door but sees something which causes her to turn right round and hurry to dining room door where she exits again, leaving door open.* CANTEL *enters from hall followed by* DESIREE, *He carries a pen and the card. He goes to sofa table, puts down card and starts to write.*)

DESIREE   I never knew it was Rosie's birthday.

CANTEL   (*as he writes*) She doesn't advertise it widely.

(CANTEL *stops writing, reaches for the champagne and grips nothing. He stares.*)

What the hell . . . ? (*Lifts cushions on sofa.*) Where's that ruddy bottle?

DESIREE   It was there.

CANTEL   (*searching*) I know it was there, but it isn't now, is it? Rosie must have nicked it. (*Shouts.*) Rosie! Rosie!

(ROSIE *enters from dining room. She wears glasses of an ornate design and a bright day dress. She carries a tray on which are the bottle of champagne, four mugs, a sugar bowl and a black top hat which stands on its head.*)

ROSIE   Don't shout. I've a bit of a head.

CANTEL   You don't say! And, other than that, how do we find ourselves this morning?

(ROSIE *puts tray down on table behind sofa.*)

ROSIE   A little better I think. I've booked in an appointment to see a nerve doctor tomorrow.

CANTEL   Sounds a good idea.

ROSIE   I've had nightmares before, woke up and thought they'd really happened, but never like this.

DESIREE	It's understandable. You've had a ghastly weekend with poor Lucy Fordyce dying in the bath.
ROSIE	That's what I keep telling myself but I didn't imagine this lump on my head, did I?
CANTEL	You had a whopper after your skirmish with the Hoover . . .
ROSIE	Oh, I wish you people would stop going on about that! Anyone can trip over a Hoover in a dark cupboard. This was different. I saw her, lying there.
DESIREE	Try to forget it. Rosie.
ROSIE	I can't. Either I did see her or I am going off me rocker.
	(CANTEL *has moved to the tray and is looking at it.*)
CANTEL	(*pointing*) What's this in aid of, Rosie?
ROSIE	Coffee for the undertaker's men. Poor things. What a deadly job.
CANTEL	Isn't it carrying respect for the dead a bit far serving them coffee in a top hat?
ROSIE	I'm not! Silly! One of them dropped his hat on the stairs.
CANTEL	(*looking closer*) Uh huh. So why have you put sugar in it?
ROSIE	What do you mean? Only a lunatic would put sugar in a top hat. (*Looks into hat.*) I did! I *am* going off me head. (*Picks up sugar bowl and turns it upside down. It is empty.*) I meant to put it into this. Tch! Lucky you noticed.

Imagine him putting his hat on again without knowing!

CANTEL   He might have landed himself a dandruff commercial.

(ROSIE *carefully tips the sugar from hat into sugar bowl.*)

ROSIE   I'm not going to tell the doctor about this.

(CANTEL *picks up the champagne.*)

CANTEL   About the champagne . . .

ROSIE   Take your sticky fingers off that. It's mine.

CANTEL   I know it's yours but how do you know it's yours?

ROSIE   Because Miss Daintee just gave it to me for me birthday.

CANTEL/   (*together*) Miss Daintee!
DESIREE

ROSIE   (*looking at label*) That's a good year. Must have cost a packet.

CANTEL   It did!

ROSIE   I think she must have a guilty conscience about something.

CANTEL   She has!

ROSIE   (*sniffing at sugar bowl*) Oh dear! Now the sugar smells of Brylcream.

CANTEL   Never mind. Nothing can make your coffee worse than it is.

ROSIE   Cheeky!

CANTEL   Happy birthday, Rosie.

(CANTEL *hands* ROSIE *the card which she reads.*)

ROSIE 'A bottle of bubbly, with love Tim Cantel'. I don't understand. What bottle?

CANTEL This one.

ROSIE But Miss Daintee . . . (*Getting it.*) She couldn't! She wouldn't . . . !

CANTEL She did.

ROSIE Really! She's getting impossible. I better take her to that doctor, too. Come along. You and me'll go and give her a piece of my mind.

(ROSIE *picks up tray.*)

CANTEL She could do with it.

(*As* CANTEL *and* ROSIE *move L,* MRS PRATT *enters from hall.*)

MRS PRATT Miss Lake, are you aware that Miss Daintee is squatting beside the gas meter with a tin opener?

ROSIE That settles it. I'll have to get rid of her.

CANTEL If you want a hit man I'll do her in for a tenner.

(ROSIE *exits into hall, passing* MRS PRATT. CANTEL *follows and pauses by* MRS PRATT.)

Not you, Mrs Pratt. I'd do you for a fiver.

(CANTEL *exits into hall, after putting champagne on sideboard.*)

MRS PRATT Detestable man. I never know what he's talking about. (*Suppresses wind.*) That haddock at breakfast was definitely off. If I get ptomaine poisoning Miss Lake will hear from my solicitor.

DESIREE Now, Mumsie . . .

MRS PRATT   Doctor Renshaw said that my next attack could
                be my last after my collapse in Bognor.

DESIREE   He was only trying to stop you overdoing it.

MRS PRATT   (*cutting in*) How long was I unconscious – in a
                coma – with you running around screaming
                'Mummy's dead'! instead of summoning an
                ambulance?

DESIREE   Well, you looked like death.

MRS PRATT   If that doctor with the bad breath hadn't been
                passing the door I probably would have
                perished. Perhaps that's what you wished. But
                I warn you there'll be precious little money.

                (MRS PRATT *goes to the sofa-table on which are
                assorted magazines and papers. She picks up
                the Radio Times.*)

DESIREE   If pennies are really short I've offered to go
                and work.

MRS PRATT   Work? At what? If you had worked harder to
                find yourself a husband . . .

DESIREE   Some men prefer a woman for her mind. One
                day I may surprise you.

                (MRS PRATT *has moved to 'her' chair, looking
                at the Radio Times as she goes.*)

MRS PRATT   Ah. The BBC are showing *Mummy's Coffin*
                again tonight. For the third time. I like that one.
                A great deal of blood.

                (MRS PRATT *sits down, freezes, utters a cry of
                pain and leaps up again. She turns, looks into
                the chair then picks up the kukri knife.*)

DESIREE   Good heavens!

MRS PRATT   I've been stabbed! Look! Blood!

DESIREE (*rushing to her*) No. It isn't blood – not yours anyway. It's dry. (*Examines* MRS PRATT *from the rear.*) Nothing torn. You're okay.

MRS PRATT I most certainly am *not*. Someone will answer for this. (*Examines knife.*) It looks foreign, It's that Chinese cook!

DESIREE He never leaves the kitchen.

MRS PRATT He probably threw it when my back was turned. He knows what I think of him.

(MRS PRATT *sits carefully.*)

Knives in the residents' lounge. This would never have happened in the old days before the Lake woman took over.

DESIREE (*awkwardly*) Mumsie, should someone . . . if there was a person . . . even if he didn't seem quite suitable, you wouldn't spoil it all like last time . . .?

(DESIREE *puts knife on desk.*)

MRS PRATT (*totally ignoring her*) I think it was a Chinaman in some restaurant who was caught putting cat food into the fish pies.

(DOCTOR ALI *enters from hall. He is a slim Pakistani of about 30, pale-skinned, good-looking. He speaks good but not perfect English. He carries a newspaper printed in Urdu. He is evidently looking for something and continues to do so during ensuing dialogue.* MRS PRATT *eyes him with hostility and speaks with meaning.*)

No, it was a Pakistani. Some people have forgotten how to say 'good morning'.

DOCTOR   Did we not hold a post mortem on the haddock
            at breakfast, Mrs Pratt? However, again good
            morning.

DESIREE   Any news yet, Doctor Ali?

DOCTOR   (*still searching*) Not yet, Miss Pratt. The post
            is late again with this go slow.

DESIREE   It'll be good news I'm sure. Isn't it wonderful,
            Mumsie? He'll be Doctor Ali, MRCP.

MRS PRATT   I have not the slightest idea what that means
            and, still less, I imagine, will the unfortunate
            Pakistanis. Are you looking for something?

DOCTOR   Yes, I . . . (*Sees knife and picks it up.*) No, I
            have it.

MRS PRATT   That is your weapon?

DOCTOR   Yes. (*Showing it.*) Kukri.

MRS PRATT   You use it for cookery?

DOCTOR   No. It is called Kukri. A Gurkha knife, I am
            finding it in Portobello Market.

MRS PRATT   And I am finding it in my chair. I sat on it.

DOCTOR   Oh, I am sorry.

MRS PRATT   You will have cause to be if tetanus sets in.

DOCTOR   Then you must let me examine you . . .

            (MRS PRATT *holds him off with her cane.*)

MRS PRATT   Young man, I would not allow my own
            physician, who is seventy-five, to examine me
            there. (*Points to blade.*) And what is that on
            the blade? Blood?

DOCTOR   (*shortly*) No. Rust. Excuse me, please.

            (DOCTOR *exits into hall.*)

MRS PRATT   That's a weird one. This course he is supposed
             to be taking is in Hammersmith, is it not?

DESIREE   What do you mean 'supposed'? It is in
             Hammersmith.

MRS PRATT   Well, *three* times in the last month Mrs
             Privett-Smith has seen him sneaking out of a
             sinister-looking house in Marylebone High
             Street, near her dressmaker's. And we all know
             what goes on in Marylebone High Street –
             illegal operations.

DESIREE   Abortions?

MRS PRATT   If you insist on using filthy language.

             (*Loud bump from above.*)

             Ha! It sounds as if those undertakers have
             dropped Miss Fordyce's coffin. I trust they'll
             have her out by luncheon. Why are they taking
             so long?

DESIREE   They've only been up there a few minutes.

MRS PRATT   In the better class of establishment they
             remove bodies by night. Too many deaths can
             give a place a bad name. Of course this is the
             trouble when one has an ex-actress attempting
             to run an hotel.

ROSIE   (*offstage*) Don't bother to change the sheets,
             Nellie. They were clean on the night before
             last.

             (ROSIE *enters from hall. She carries the two
             silver ornaments and a sheaf of cut flowers in
             a cellophane wrapping and wears her
             spectacles perched in her hair above her
             forehead. They must be prominently displayed.
             She places ornaments on occasional table.*)

ROSIE   Has anyone seen me glasses?

(Mrs Pratt *makes a disgusted gesture and turns away.* Desiree *smiles, shakes her head and points a finger upwards, "No, I've looked upstairs . . ."*)

DESIREE   On your head, Rosie dear!

ROSIE   (*finding them*) Now whoever put them there? (*Puts them on.*) Someone has sent me a lovely bunch of flowers for my birthday and I couldn't see to read the card.

DESIREE   Yes, you naughty girl. You never told us it was your birthday.

(ROSIE *tears off the cellophane wrapping and shoves the flowers into the empty vase.*)

ROSIE   I try to forget it, love. Now whoever remembered . . . ? (*She looks at the card attached to the now crumpled cellophane. Reads.*) 'From Agnes and Desiree Pratt'. Oh! It was you two and pretending you didn't know! Aren't you sweet?

MRS PRATT   I didn't send you flowers!

ROSIE   Yes, you did! (*Reading again.*) "With deepest sympathy". (*Puzzled.*) Deepest sympathy?

MRS PRATT   (*rising*) You fool! (*Points upwards with cane.*) Those were for the corpse – not you!

ROSIE   Oh, dear!

DESIREE   Never mind. It was just a thought.

ROSIE   And a very sweet thought. (*Kisses* DESIREE.) Thank you, love.

MRS PRATT   Forget the 'thank you loves'! If you keep Miss Fordyce's flowers you will pay for them. Flowers cost money.

Rosie	(*grimacing behind her back*) All right! All right! (*To* Desiree.) Talking of money, you didn't by chance take any out of Lucy Fordyce's room?
Mrs Pratt	⸌How dare you!
Rosie	For safekeeping, you stup – (*Controls herself, addresses* Desiree *again.*) She generally kept quite a tidy sum but I couldn't find a trace of any money; been through the room twice. Perhaps Miss Daintee took it.
Desiree	So that's what you were doing in Lucy's room this morning?
Rosie	That – and something else, very strange . . .
Desiree	What?
Rosie	No, forget it.
Mrs Pratt	A splendid idea. And if Miss Fordyce's money is missing you might care to ask a few searching questions of that Pakistani doctor.
Desiree	Mumsie! Why?
Mrs Pratt	After she collapsed in the bath it was he who attended her and he owes you three months' board, does he not?
Rosie	Really, Mrs Pitt . . .
Mrs Pratt	*Pratt* for goodness sake! You have known me for five years and still you get it wrong.
	(Rosie *hears something and glances out of hall door.*)
Rosie	They're bringing the poor soul down now.
Mrs Pratt	About time. I was just remarking you should remove your cadavers by night.
Rosie	Miss Fordyce couldn't go by night.

MRS PRATT   She could if you had taken the trouble to
             organise it. The Burlingworth opposite always
             do and their mortality rate is just as high as
             ours.

ROSIE   Lucy Fordyce is catching a train, remember?
             She's not due at the crematorium in Brighton
             until 2.30 and you can't leave a coffin in the
             left luggage, can you?

MRS PRATT   I don't know. I've never tried.

DESIREE   I wonder why Fordy wanted to be cremated in
             Brighton with Golders Green so near?

MRS PRATT   Because she had more sense than one gave her
             credit for. I wouldn't be seen dead in Golders
             Green.

ROSIE   (*moves to window, looks out*) You're right. It is
             a bit of showing-up having a hearse at the
             door. Still it is a Daimler.

MRS PRATT   The Pratts have always gone by Rolls Royce.
             Even our butler went by Rolls Royce. I shall
             insist upon a Rolls when my time comes.

ROSIE   I'll order you one with the greatest of pleasure.

             (MRS PRATT *darts* ROSIE *a sharp look but* ROSIE
             keeps a straight face.)

DESIREE   (*looking out of window*) Here she comes.

             (MRS PRATT *joins* ROSIE *at window.*)

MRS PRATT   My word! They are making heavy weather with
             that coffin. You'd think she weighted a ton
             instead of six stone something.

ROSIE   And she'd put on weight. She was a bag of
             bones when she first came here – looked like
             death. This place did her the world of good, the
             world of good.

MRS PRATT   Oh, yes! Look at her now!

DESIREE   Poor little Fordy. She always said she wanted to die at sea.

ROSIE   (*sighs*) Yes, but I suppose doing it in the bath was the next best thing. (*Another sigh.*) She made a lovely corpse.

(DESIREE *goes and sits on sofa.*)

MRS PRATT   (*sarcasm*) Talking of corpses, has Mrs Privett-Smith returned from the dead yet?

ROSIE   Save your sarcasm, Mrs Potter. (*Points to key rack.*) Her key's not back, is it? It's funny she always says where she's going but this time she didn't; and, when I looked into her room this morning, I saw she'd packed enough clothes for a month. Something's up, I feel it.

MRS PRATT   (*more heavy sarcasm*) I seem to recall standing here at 2.00 am this morning with you insisting you had seen her dead.

ROSIE   (*strident, waving her arms*) All right! All right! So I had one of me turns; but it could have been a premonition. I am physic, you know.

MRS PRATT   I assume you mean psychic.

ROSIE   That's what I said. Did I tell you about that time I was playing the Grand Theatre, Leeds? (*Carries straight on.*) I dreamed there was an earthquake and the whole theatre fell in. And what happened next night – *the very next night?*

MRS PRATT   All right, what?

ROSIE   I slipped in the toilet and broke my collarbone.

MRS PRATT   Was there an earthquake in the toilet?

ROSIE   No.

MRS PRATT   Then that's the stupidest thing I ever heard.
             Psychic!

ROSIE   Well, if something has happened to Mrs
             Privett-Thing, just remember this conversation.

MRS PRATT   She could have had a seizure of some kind.
             She's been looking very pink of late.

ROSIE   Nonsense! Her old friend Colonel
             Whatsisname-Forbes sent her a little pot of
             rouge from Bournemouth. She's been using
             that.

MRS PRATT   He would. Disgusting old man.

ROSIE   Oh, be quiet you vicious woman!

MRS PRATT   I am not accustomed to being called vicious,
             Miss Lake. I shall write to my solicitor this
             afternoon.

ROSIE   Give him my regards.

MRS PRATT   (*regally*) I would not demean myself by
             mentioning your name. (*Moves towards hall
             door.*) By the way, in future, we shall be taking
             our meals at Miss Fordyce's old table.

ROSIE   You can't. Miss Daintee has already bagged it.

MRS PRATT   *Bagged it?* This is not a girls' school and I
             placed my pot of marmalade upon it after
             breakfast this morning.

ROSIE   This is my hotel and no one takes claims with
             pratts of marmalade, Mrs Potts.

MRS PRATT   (*rising*) I refuse to discuss the matter. Either I
             take my luncheon at that table or my luggage is
             moved to the Burlingworth this afternoon.

             (MRS PRATT *exits regally into hall.*)

ROSIE	Old cow!
DESIREE	Rosie!
	(ROSIE *gives a guilty start and swings round to see* DESIREE *on sofa.*)
ROSIE	Whoops! I forgot you were there. Forgive me, love. I'm not myself this morning.
DESIREE	That's okay! I know Mumsie can be a bit of a trial, but . . .
ROSIE	Even so, I can't afford to lose anyone else; so she can have the blessed table. I'll shift Miss Daintee to Whatyamacallit's table as soon as he leaves.
DESIREE	Whatyamacallit?
ROSIE	You now the Whatsit-Scoutmaster.
DESIREE	There's no Scoutmaster here . . .
ROSIE	I mean the thingy-Squadron Leader.
	(DESIREE *visibly stiffens.*)
DESIREE	Tim Cantel? He's leaving?
ROSIE	Very soon.
DESIREE	(*flustered, incoherent*) How do you know? When did he tell you?
ROSIE	Last night when I'd come down to look for the cat and there was this awful business; and that's another worry.
DESIREE	What happened?
ROSIE	I urched around, hardly able to stand, making t'1e most peculiar noises.
DESIREE	Good heavens!

ROSIE   (*nods*) Then squatted down, looked up at me
                pathetically and mewed.

DESIREE   Not the cat! The Squadron Leader. What did he
                say?

ROSIE   Oh! Something about packing up at the flying
                club because he'd landed a smashing new job
                and would be leaving any minute. I wasn't
                really listening . . .

DESIREE   Try to remember. Did he say anything else?

ROSIE   Only made me swear not to tell a living soul.
                (*Reacts.*) Oh! Oh, dear! Well, you don't count.
                You're discreet. I wouldn't mention it, though,
                unless he does.

                (DOCTOR *enters from hall, moves to near
                telephone and key rack.* DESIREE *moves
                towards hall door, deeply worried.*)

DESIREE   No, of course I won't, though I'm sure he'll tell
                me. I mean, he's bound to.

                (DESIREE *exits into hall.* ROSIE *moves to
                sideboard and pours a drink. She thus has her
                back to the* DOCTOR *and does not see him hang
                a front door key on an empty hook on the
                rack.*)

ROSIE   If you ask me she's one of the reasons why
                he's leaving. She's been making sheep's eyes
                at him for weeks, poor thing.

DOCTOR   (*moves from rack*) Who is leaving?

ROSIE   The Squadron Leader. Oh! It's supposed to be
                a secret, but I can tell you, because you're
                discreet, Care for a drink, doctor?

DOCTOR   Thank you, no. I never drink, as you will
                remember. (*Produces some banknotes from his
                pocket.*) I have the money I am owing you.

ROSIE   Oh, not to bother.

(*Despite the disclaimer* ROSIE *takes it quickly.*)

DOCTOR   It is just arriving. You have been too kind. I will never forget.

ROSIE   Ah, say no more. Help yourself to a drink.

DOCTOR   (*patiently*) Thank you, no. I never drink as you will remember.

(DOCTOR *moves back towards hall door.*)

ROSIE   I shouldn't be either. I only drink at weekends as a rule but I'm making this a long weekend.

(DOCTOR *exits into hall.* ROSIE *moves over towards the alcove and stands with her back to the door, looking down at the spot where she has seen the body. She sighs, shakes her head, then suddenly reacts as she notices something on the key rack. It is the key just put there by the* DOCTOR. *With a shaky hand she takes key off the hook and looks at it. She looks at the spot where the body was.*)

She did come back! She *was* here!

(MARK *enters from hall. He almost closes door behind him then tiptoes silently towards* ROSIE, *whose back is to him. With what intent we do not know he raises both hands and stretches them out towards* ROSIE'S *neck. Perhaps through sixth sense or perhaps she sees something out of the corner of her eye,* ROSIE *turns, sees the apparently threatening hands, screams loudly and wallops* MARK *hard in the midriff. He cries out, doubles up sinks on his knees to the floor.*)

ROSIE   (*strident*) What are you doing?

MARK   (*gasping*) I was about to kiss the back of your neck and wish you a happy birthday.

ROSIE   Don't creep up on people!

             (MARK *has risen to his feet.*)

MARK   I won't again, I promise.

             (DOCTOR *and* CANTEL *enter together from hall.*)

CANTEL   What's happened? Someone yelled.

MARK   Rosie's taken up karate. Hiya! Ya! Doing well
             for a beginner.

ROSIE   I'm sorry, Mark love. I really am, but you see,
             something's happened. I know you all think I'm
             dotty; but Mrs Privett-Smith did come back last
             night. I did see her lying there and now I can
             prove it.

MARK   You didn't find the body?

ROSIE   (*raising key*) No this. Her front door key.

CANTEL   How do you know it's hers?

ROSIE   There is only two of them. Five minutes ago I
             looked at that rack and there was just one. Now
             there's two.

MARK   Not so fast, Rosie. A couple of weeks ago you
             lost a front door key.

ROSIE   All right, so what did it do? Walk back on its
             own and hang itself up on the hook?

MARK   Somebody presumably hung it up.

ROSIE   Who? If someone found a key why didn't they
             say so? Why sneak it back?

DOCTOR   (*nervously*) I am putting key on rack a few
             minutes ago.

             (*All look at* DOCTOR.)

ROSIE   Why?

DOCTOR	Because this is where you are keeping keys, isn't it?
ROSIE	But why didn't you say something?
DOCTOR	It did not seem important. I did not know it was Mrs Privett-Smith's.
CANTEL	Where did you find it?
DOCTOR	In passage upstairs.
ROSIE	Outside her room?
DOCTOR	(*to* MARK) No, outside your room, Mr Anderson.

(ROSIE *and* CANTEL *look at* MARK.)

MARK	Don't look at me. (*To* ROSIE.) It's almost certainly the one you lost days ago.
ROSIE	No. It's hers. I feel it in my bones.
MARK	Let's forget your bones, Rosie, and stick to facts. It has to be one of three explanations. First one, this is the key you lost two weeks ago and Mrs Privett-Smith is alive, well and probably having it away with old Colonel Forbes in Bournemouth.
CANTEL	I'll go along with that one.
ROSIE	No, I don't believe that.
MARK	Okay. Explanation two. Mrs Privett-Smith arrives back here last night and lets herself in with this key. She is accompanied by a man.
ROSIE	Who says so?
MARK	According to you someone killed her and slugged you. Right?
ROSIE	Yes.

MARK   Before you recover and sound the alarm he picks up the body and carries it out into Queen's Gate Grove, perhaps to a car . . .

ROSIE   Yes. That makes sense.

CANTEL   No, it doesn't. I was outside untying that ruddy trunk from the top of my car. No one came out.

MARK   So he used the back door.

ROSIE   No. The back door was bolted from the inside. I checked that.

MARK   Good! So do we all agree that explanation two is a non-starter?

ROSIE   Yes, Yes. That's right.

MARK   Which leaves explanation three. Mrs Privett-Smith arrives back, lets herself in, perhaps with a man or perhaps alone. She is killed and Rosie is slugged but nobody leaves the hotel. This means that her body is still here somewhere – *and so is the murderer*.

ROSIE   Oh!

MARK   (*smiles*) Oh, indeed! The plot thickens, doesn't it? Unless the killer is a stranger and is hiding in a cupboard he has to be one of four men. Chinese Cookie, Cantel, the doctor or me.

ROSIE   Oh, don't be daft!

MARK   Come on, Rosie! This is your story and you must stick with it.

CANTEL   He's right, Rosie.

ROSIE   That cook hasn't the strength to pull the skin off a rice pudding and why would any of you three want to kill Mrs Privett-Thing?

MARK	Motive is immaterial. We all had the opportunity.
ROSIE	(*to* CANTEL) You didn't. You didn't come in until after it was over.
CANTEL	Who's to say I didn't clout you, slip out of the front door and then come back with the trunk? Maybe her body was actually in the trunk.
ROSIE	You told me to look inside!
CANTEL	But you didn't did you? (*Gestures alcove.*) Feel free now, if you like.
ROSIE	Getaway. You wouldn't be so stupid . . .
DOCTOR	(*suddenly*) And I think this is a stupid game.
CANTEL	Maybe, doc, but Anderson is right. Any of us *could* have done it.
DOCTOR	Why am I wanting to kill this woman?
CANTEL	As he said the motive isn't important; but we're all equally suspect. Take you. You had the key. You put it back. You also had one hell of a row with old Privett-Smith last Thursday night . . .
DOCTOR	That is a lie!
CANTEL	(*shrugs*) That's *your* story, old son. You stick to it.
DOCTOR	(*advancing, fists clenched*) You be careful . . .
MARK	(*intervening*) Now! Now! Nobody is making any accusations. Just making a point.
DOCTOR	And I am telling you that woman is alive.
	(DOCTOR *turns angrily away, goes to sofa and ostentatiously picks up his Urdu newspaper which he reads.*)

MARK   (*to* ROSIE) Rosie, the man you say slugged you.
           Have you any idea what he looked like?

ROSIE   No, it was all so quick, but I get a sort of
           feeling that I might remember . . .

CANTEL   If you don't mind my saying so that was a very
           unwise remark.

ROSIE   Why?

CANTEL   If one of us is the killer he'll stick a knife in
           your back at his first opportunity.

           (ROSIE'S *legs nearly give. She has to support
           herself against the high-backed chair.*)

ROSIE   (*dry voice*) I think I like explanation number
           one. You know, the one that says I imagined
           the whole thing.

CANTEL   (*grins*) So do we! Right Anderson?

MARK   (*also grins*) Right! Sorry Rosie. It was the best
           way to make you see sense.

ROSIE   I suppose half my trouble is not wanting to
           admit I'm going round the bend.

CANTEL   You'll be all right!

ROSIE   I'm not so sure. Doctor, you'd know. I mean
           you've come across cases like this.

           (DOCTOR *lowers paper, looks at her.*)

           It didn't end there last night, you see. After
           Tim had gone up I let poor Raggles in. She was
           in a dreadful state. That ginger Tom from the
           Burlingworth had been at her. I've a good mind
           to sue them.

CANTEL   What for? Maintenance?

ROSIE	Shut up. I gave her a cuddle, some milk and put her to bed. Then I went upstairs and, as I passed Lucy Fordyce's door, I heard her moving about inside her room.
MARK	Last night!
DOCTOR	Miss Lake! Miss Fordyce died on Saturday morning, remember?
ROSIE	Of course I remember now; but I didn't remember then. It shows you the state I was in. Forgetting she was dead and thinking she might not be feeling well, I knocked on the door. There was a distinct 'thump' like something being dropped; but no answer.
MARK	Then what?
ROSIE	I opened the door and there was her coffin but nobody else in the room.
CANTEL	You'd have had a nasty shock if she had been there.
ROSIE	Naturally, as soon as I saw the coffin it all came back to me but what made the thump? What do you think about that, doctor?
DOCTOR	That you should keep such experiences to yourself, Miss Lake. People might misunderstand.
ROSIE	That's what I thought you'd think. I'm terrified they'll lock me up.

(*A gong booms sonorously for lunch. Almost instantly* MISS DAINTEE *enters from hall. She makes a bee-line for dining room door. Hot on her heels come* MRS PRATT *and* DESIREE. *The two old ladies collide and jostle each other in the doorway, allowing* DESIREE *to glide through into dining room.*)

MRS PRATT   Oh, no you don't, Miss Daintee! Desiree! Get
                   that table!

                   (MRS PRATT *and* MISS DAINTEE *exit into dining
                   room*.)

CANTEL   One day someone will get killed in the rush.
                   (*Offstage front doorbell rings*.)

ROSIE   Oh, that'll be the new arrival. Only staying a
                   couple of nights.

                   (ROSIE *exits into hall*.)

DOCTOR   Monday. Curry. I must hurry.

                   (DOCTOR *moves towards dining room door and
                   exits*.)

CANTEL   A poet yet! (*Calls out*.) Yes, eat it while it's
                   hot.

MARK   Well, what do you make of all this?

CANTEL   Same as you. The sooner our Rosie sees her
                   shrink the better. (*Pause*.) At the same time . . .

MARK   Yes?

CANTEL   Young Doc Ali over-reacted a bit, I thought –
                   and he was giving the Privett absolute hell last
                   Thursday night.

                   (ROSIE *enters from hall, accompanied by* JEAN
                   SMITH, *an extremely attractive young girl. She
                   carries a small overnight bag. She looks shy
                   and nervous*.)

ROSIE   This is the lounge where you can lounge.

JEAN   Very nice.

ROSIE   Just a bit careful which chair you sit in.

JEAN   Why?

CANTEL	Some bite and others collapse.
ROSIE	(*hits him with her fan*) Oh, be quiet, Tim! (*To* JEAN.) The older residents sort of reserve certain chairs for themselves. Now, this is Scoutmaster Cantel who teaches people to fly now he's retired from the Army. Miss Jean Smith.
CANTEL	(*shaking* JEAN'S *hand*) Smith, eh? A likely story.
JEAN	How do you do?
ROSIE	(*to* JEAN) And you don't want to take any notice of him. This is Mr Mark Anderson, the actor.
JEAN	An actor?
ROSIE	Very famous. Or will be, one day.
MARK	(*shakes* JEAN'S *hand*) And you don't want to take any notice of her either.
ROSIE	(*to* JEAN) You'll be wanting lunch, I'll just show you quickly to your room . . . the girl should have got it ready, though the previous resident was only taken to Brighton half an hour ago.
CANTEL	Blimey, Rosie! You haven't . . .
ROSIE	(*cuts in loudly*) Why aren't you two eating? Your soup will get hot. (*To* JEAN.) It's just up the stairs, dear. I'll follow you in a moment.
	(ROSIE *ushers* JEAN *out, pauses, looks back.*)
ROSIE	(*hissing*) Don't you say a word about that room. She's young and it might give her nightmares.
MARK	We'll be as silent as the grave.

CANTEL   (*laughs*) Not bad! (*Quietly to* ROSIE.) Hey,
            Rosie. You haven't mentioned to anybody what
            I told you last night?

ROSIE   About your *leaving?* No, love. Haven't
            breathed a word to a soul.

CANTEL   Oh thanks! (*Indicating* MARK.) What about
            him? He's stone deaf, is he?

ROSIE   Mark doesn't count. He's discreet aren't you
            dear?

            (ROSIE *exits into hall with* MARK. DESIREE
            enters hurriedly from dining room intercepting
            CANTEL *as he goes to enter it.*)

DESIREE   Timmy.

CANTEL   (*cautiously*) Yes?

DESIREE   What's this about your leaving?

CANTEL   (*exploding*) Who the hell told you?

DESIREE   Rosie.

CANTEL   I'll murder that woman.

DESIREE   Why didn't you tell me?

CANTEL   Only fixed it this weekend and I haven't had a
            chance.

DESIREE   You did. In here, just now.

CANTEL   I was going to tell you, when we had more time.

DESIREE   I see. Where are you going?

CANTEL   Um . . . Bermuda.

DESIREE   Bermuda!

CANTEL   I've landed a good job, Desiree. Couldn't
            possibly turn it down.

DESIREE   Of course not. Super. I'm glad for you, dear.

CANTEL	Thanks. Tell you more about it later. Better get some lunch.

(CANTEL *moves as if to go. She follows and stops him near sofa.*)

DESIREE	Timmy, you weren't thinking of going off without telling me?
CANTEL	(*awkwardly*) No . . . no . . .
DESIREE	So when you say you're leaving, it could be *us* leaving . . . ?
CANTEL	(*nearly writhing*) Well, I mean . . . your mother. You probably wouldn't want to leave her just like that, without warning.

(DESIREE *suddenly seizes him and throws him on to the sofa, speaking passionately.*)

DESIREE	Oh, yes! Yes! Nothing matters except us. I'd leave here tonight for the end of the world to be with you. Face up to it darling. We love each other. I want you! I want you!

(*She climbs all over him, embraces him passionately.* ROSIE *enters from hall and stares, amazed. Then wheels right round without stopping and exits again as* CANTEL *fights himself clear. Neither of them has seen* ROSIE.)

CANTEL	For God's sake girl! This is a public room!
DESIREE	I'm sorry.
CANTEL	I should damn well think so. What would people think?
DESIREE	I don't care what people think. I care what you think.

CANTEL   Look, Desiree, I've been trying to drop you the
                  hint for days. The fact that we hopped into bed
                  for half an hour does not constitute a contract
                  of any kind.

DESIREE   B-but not ten minutes ago we were discussing
                  our future . . .

CANTEL   Correction. You were. From the moment it
                  happened you've been putting on the pressure,
                  driving me into a corner.

DESIREE   Are you always as cruel as this?

CANTEL   Frankly, I don't have to be.

                  (DESIREE *exits to hall in tears.*)

CANTEL   (*shaken*) Jeez . . !

                  (CANTEL *notices* ROSIE's *bottle on the
                  sideboard. Unable to resist it he grabs it and
                  pours himself a drink. He raises the glass to
                  his lips as* ROSIE *and* JEAN SMITH *enter from
                  hall.* CANTEL *chokes.*)

ROSIE   Tim, will show you, Miss Brown . . .

JEAN   Smith.

ROSIE   Me and names! Now, what was it I wanted you
                  to show her?

CANTEL   I shudder to think.

ROSIE   The dining room! Show her to the dining room.
                  I must go. Raggles is either having a fit or
                  asking to go out.

                  (ROSIE *exits, closing hall door.*)

CANTEL   (*to* JEAN) Have no fear. She wasn't talking
                  about one of the residents. They do have fits
                  but Raggles is an old cat. (*He gestures towards
                  dining room door.*) This way Miss Brown – or
                  is it Miss Smith?

JEAN	Either will do, Squadron Leader . . . or is it Scoutmaster?
	(CANTEL *laughs, holds out his arms.* JEAN *runs forward and they embrace briefly but passionately.*)
CANTEL	Oh, how I needed that!
	(JEAN *keeps her arms round him. They embrace again.* ROSIE *enters from hall and is amazed, then wheels right round and exits, once again without stopping, Neither of them see* ROSIE.)
CANTEL	Keep it for tonight, darling. A bit public here.
	(CANTEL *indicates the dining room where they exit. A pause, then* ROSIE *puts her head through the hall door. She looks dazed. She enters and stands just inside the room, her mouth agape. She picks up the bottle of whisky.* MARK *enters and notices her expression.*)
MARK	Something wrong?
ROSIE	It's getting worse.
MARK	What is?
ROSIE	Me. (*Taps her head.*) I march in here and see Desiree raping the Squadron Leader on the couch . . .
MARK	What!
ROSIE	Oh, that's nothing! Then I come in again and the Squadron Leader's climbing over that new girl he only met two minutes before. (*Sees* MARK *looking at the bottle.*) And I haven't touched a drop!
MARK	Well, lively bodies are better than dead ones.

(MARK *waves and exits into dining room.* ROSIE *looks more closely at bottle.*)

ROSIE   Hey! Someone's been at this and that's not my imagination.   .

(ROSIE *picks up a pencil and marks the bottle.* DESIREE *enters from hall, wearing a raincoat, her face blotched with tears.*)

DESIREE   If you see Mummy tell her I don't want any lunch and have gone for a walk.

ROSIE   What's the matter, love? Oh, I know. He turned you down.

DESIREE   Eh?

ROSIE   Forget I said that. I didn't see a thing.

DESIREE   Rosie, can I talk to you in confidence?

ROSIE   If you can't talk to *me* in confidence, who can you talk to? (ROSIE *pushes* DESIREE *into sofa and sits beside her.*) Now, what's the trouble?

DESIREE   What would you do if you discovered you were going to have a baby?

ROSIE   Call up the Guinness Book of Records. It would be the second miraculous conception in history. (*A delayed reaction.*) What are you trying to say?

DESIREE   I'm late and I felt very sick this morning.

ROSIE   (*incredulous*) You! You have . . . who with?

DESIREE   If I tell you, do you swear not to say anything to him or anyone?

ROSIE   (*she means it*) Trust me.

DESIREE   It was Timmy, (ROSIE *looks blank.*) Tim Cantel. The Squadron Leader.

ROSIE	(*astounded*) I don't believe it! Was he drunk?
DESIREE	(*bridling*) No! Of course he wasn't!
ROSIE	Sorry, love. I didn't mean . . . I'm just surprised . . . didn't think you were quite his type. (*After thought.*) *Gorgeous* though you are.
DESIREE	If I told him about this he'd do the right thing and ask me to marry him.
ROSIE	You think so?
DESIREE	Yes and I don't want to get married under those circumstances. That's why I want to, you know, get rid of it. Do you think Doctor Ali might help?
ROSIE	Now that's a good idea! He's bound to know the ropes.
DESIREE	That's what Mummy said.
ROSIE	(*astonished*) Your mother knows?
DESIREE	Oh, no! And she mustn't. That's why I must do it quietly, and not legally. If she found out the shock could kill her.
	(DOCTOR *enters from dining room.* ROSIE *moves UL.*)
ROSIE	Well I must look for that cat. Can't find her anywhere.
	(ROSIE *gives* DESIREE *an encouraging wink and exits into hall.*)
DESIREE	Can you spare me a moment, doctor?
DOCTOR	Of course.
DESIREE	I'm in a spot of trouble; probably preggers.
DOCTOR	Preggers?

DESIREE	Pregnant. (DOCTOR *gives an astonished start*.) I – ah – wondered if you could help?
DOCTOR	(*nods*) I am advising you in any way I can.
DESIREE	Oh, thank goodness! Lucky I talked to Mummy or I'd never have had the nerve to broach it.
DOCTOR	It is not an unusual condition, Miss Pratt.
DESIREE	It is for me! I'm only about three weeks gone. I mean, could the operation be done quietly in a day so that I could come back here with no one ever knowing?
DOCTOR	If there were no complications.
DESIREE	And it would be Marylebone High Street, of course.
	(DOCTOR *gives a distinct start*.)
DOCTOR	What do you know of Marylebone High Street?
DESIREE	Only that's where I'm told you operate. (*Confidentially*.) Don't worry. I think you people render a great service.
DOCTOR	Who is telling you this?
DESIREE	Mummy. She got it from Mrs Privett-Smith. I'm afraid old Privy spotted you there several times.
DOCTOR	Did she? And your mother is telling you that this is where I am carrying out illegal operations.
DESIREE	(*sensing hostility*) Well, sort of. They assumed . . .
DOCTOR	(*harsh, grim*) I am sorry to disappoint you. I am not in practice here, legal or illegal.
DESIREE	But you said you . . .

DOCTOR   You are mistaken. I said nothing.

(DESIREE *runs forward and seizes him by the arms, pulling him close to her.*)

DESIREE   Don't turn me down please . . . (ROSIE *enters, unseen by them, from hall. For the third time she wheels round and staggers out again. She wears a pair of less gaudy spectacles.*) I need you!

(DOCTOR *roughly pushes* DESIREE *away.*)

DOCTOR   I have nothing to add, Miss Pratt. I will not discuss this any more.

(DESIREE *sobs and runs to hall door and exits.* DOCTOR *goes to telephone and dials a number.*)

(*into telephone*) Mohammet? Rashid here. I have another problem. A Mrs Pratt. Yes, just as with Mrs Privett-Smith. We may have to deal with her in the same way. Well, it worked with Mrs Privett-Smith, no?

(MRS PRATT *enters from dining room and closes door.* DOCTOR *sees her.*)

I can't talk more now. I will call again. (DOCTOR *hangs up.*)

MRS PRATT Secrets?

(DOCTOR *ignores this.* MRS PRATT *moves towards hall door.*)

The curry was edible. I ate as discreetly as possible. However, we shall see.

DOCTOR   (*sharply*) Do not leave, Mrs Pratt.

MRS PRATT I beg your pardon?

(DOCTOR *advances on her, his voice quiet but menacing. His eyes gaze at her fiercely.*)

DOCTOR   I am advising no more talk of my private life, of
                  Marylebone High Street, of anything about me.
                  This is a dangerous game – as your friend Mrs
                  Privett-Smith found out.

MRS PRATT   She's no friend . . . (*Reacts.*) What about Mrs
                  Privett-Smith?

DOCTOR   She also went too far. I will not warn you again.

                  (DOCTOR *exits into hall.* MRS PRATT, *visibly
                  shaken, slumps down in tub chair. She opens
                  her mouth, makes a choking noise, then fails
                  back in the chair, her eyes staring and her
                  mouth agape. She remains frozen in this
                  position. She could be dead.* ROSIE *cautiously
                  enters from hall, sees* MRS PRATT'S *condition.*)

ROSIE   Mrs Proops!

                  (MARK *enters from dining room.*)

                  Quick! Mrs Thing! She's dead! Desiree warned
                  me it might happen.

                  (*They both go to* MRS PRATT. MRS PRATT *moves,
                  makes a strangled noise.*)

MARK   No way is she dead.

MRS PRATT   Police! Get the police! That doctor. Threatened
                  my life and you were right he has done away
                  with Mrs Privett-Smith. He killed her.

ROSIE   Now, now, Mrs Pruit. You're not yourself.

MRS PRATT   (*recovering fast*) I am myself. And the name is
                  Pratt. His eyes were blazing, his teeth were
                  bared and he warned me I would suffer the
                  same fate as Muriel Privett-Smith.

MARK   But why?

MRS PRATT   How should I know?

| MARK | You must have said something to trigger him off. I mean one doesn't discuss the weather then suddenly say. 'Oh by the way, I've wasted Mrs Privett-Smith'. |

MRS PRATT That is exactly what did happen. I made a remark about luncheon and he went berserk. He wants to kill me.

ROSIE (*an idea*) You said something insulting about curries!

MRS PRATT No! He said 'You're wondering what happened to Mrs Privett-Smith, well, she also went too far with me'.

MARK Also? Then you *did* say something to rile him.

MRS PRATT I said absolutely nothing. It is true that Mrs Privett-Smith did suspect he carried out illegal operations.

ROSIE That's it! Now I've got it. You were telling him about Desiree being in the club.

MRS PRATT Club? What club?

ROSIE Oh, come on, love! One in the oven.

MRS PRATT One in the oven?

ROSIE Pregnant!

(*Once more* MRS PRATT *gives a silent scream. She slumps back in the frozen position again, looking dead, mouth open.*)

MARK (*to* ROSIE) Your big mouth!

ROSIE I thought she knew. Now I *have* killed her. (*Flaps.*) Doctor! Doctor! Oh no! He wants to kill her. I know! Give her the kiss of life, Mark. (MARK *hastily moves away.* ROSIE *catches him and drags him back.*) I can't afford to lose another – even her.

(*As* MARK *leans over* MRS PRATT, *she opens her eyes and screams.*)

MRS PRATT Aaaaah! Get away from me! (MARK *straightens up sharply.* MRS PRATT *sits up, recovering fast.*) That oriental seduced her. I'll have him struck off.

ROSIE No! No! It wasn't the doctor. It was the Squadron Leader. (MRS PRATT *gasps, goes rigid.*) Oh! Perhaps I shouldn't have said that, either.

(MRS PRATT *goes into another attack and looks deader than ever.*)

MARK You seem determined to finish her off . . . (*Pats* MRS PRATT'S *cheek.*) It's all right, Mrs Pratt. You're all right.

(MRS PRATT *recovers again.*)

MRS PRATT (*hoarsely*) He will pay for this.

ROSIE I'm sure he will. He's a perfect gent. He must have had a temporary aberration. Now, upstairs with you and lie down.

(ROSIE *helps* MRS PRATT *up and towards hall door. None of them notice* JEAN SMITH, *who appears in dining room doorway, looking over her shoulder as if waiting for someone.* JEAN *thus overhears their conversation.*)

MRS PRATT (*to* ROSIE) I don't wish to lie down but I should like to use the telephone in your office to call my solicitor about that cad Cantel.

(ROSIE *and* MRS PRATT *exit into hall.* CANTEL *enters from dining room.*)

CANTEL Starting to rain. (*To* JEAN.) Miss Smith, I have to go out so I'll drive you to Waterloo.

JEAN	Please, don't bother.
CANTEL	Pleasure. I'll just nip upstairs and get a mac. Won't be a second.
	(CANTEL *exits into hall.*)
MARK	Leaving us so soon?
JEAN	I just finished a job up north and am going to my parents' house in the country to collect some more clothes.
MARK	What are you doing in London?
JEAN	I – hope to get a job as a secretary. Temping, you know. (*Changing subject.*) So you're an actor?
MARK	So I tell myself.
JEAN	Doing anything at the moment?
MARK	Yes, resting.
JEAN	What was your last job?
MARK	Rep, last summer at Worthing.
JEAN	(*reacts*) Worthing!
MARK	(*a hint of unease*) Yes. You know it?
JEAN	I had a friend in the company and visited her a couple of times.
MARK	Last summer?
JEAN	No, two years ago.
MARK	(*relaxes*) Pity. A year later and we might have met sooner.
JEAN	Yes. (*Changing tack again.*) What was that strange old woman on about?

MARK   (*laughs*) You meet life in the raw at the
            Delamere. Our Squadron Leader has been
            trifling with her daughter, Desiree, who claims
            to be pregnant.

JEAN   (*hotly*) That's ridiculous!

            (JEAN *sits, puts her handbag down behind sofa
            and ostentatiously picks up a magazine from
            sofa called 'Knitting World'.*)

MARK   Did I say something to annoy you?

JEAN   (*behind magazine*) I dislike petty gossip.

MARK   You did ask. (*No answer.*) Do put 'Knitting
            World' down for a second – or do you have a
            little secret, too?

            (JEAN *lowers magazine and glares at him.*)

MARK   Could I offer you a word of advice?

JEAN   No, thank you.

            (JEAN *puts magazine aside, rises and exits into
            hall, leaving her handbag behind.* MARK
            shrugs, then his eyes fall on JEAN'S *handbag.
            He moves quickly, furtively starts to examine
            the contents. He flips through the pages of a
            diary. He then takes out a bundle of
            banknotes, looks at them.*)

JEAN   (*off stage*) I think I left it in the lounge.

            (MARK *hastily drops the banknotes back and
            closes the bag.* CANTEL *and* JEAN *enter.* MARK
            holds out the bag to JEAN.)

MARK   Yours, I think?

JEAN   (*taking it*) Thank you.

MARK   Don't mention it. Happy landings, Squadron
            Leader.

            (MARK *exits to hall.*)

CANTEL	Anything missing from your bag?
JEAN	Why . . . ?
CANTEL	I thought he looked shifty and he is skint.

(JEAN *opens bag, looks inside.*)

JEAN	No. It's all right. Tim, have you and he come up against each other?
CANTEL	How do you mean?
JEAN	For no apparent reason he talked about you and someone called Desiree.
CANTEL	(*a beat*) Oh?
JEAN	Well? Is it true?
CANTEL	Don't know what he said, do I?
JEAN	That you'd been fooling around with her and that she was pregnant.
CANTEL	(*grievous shock*) Pregnant! Bloody hell! What did I do to deserve this?
JEAN	(*half laugh*) Rather a rhetorical question surely? It's obvious what you did.
CANTEL	Darling, it was before we met.
JEAN	I should damn well hope so.
CANTEL	It was just a one night stand; no, not even that. I came in, completely tanked and . . .
JEAN	Spare me the details. I just can't understand why you bring me here if she . . .
CANTEL	I didn't expect repercussions. Quite frankly, I thought she'd be grateful. And as to clicking . . . I still can't believe it.

(JEAN *sits in a high-back chair.*)

JEAN   We only have that man's word. And about him,
              you said he was an actor. Well, I don't believe
              he is.

CANTEL   Why?

JEAN   He just had a bit of bad luck. He told me he was
              in rep at Worthing last summer.

CANTEL   (*reacts*) But that means you and he . . .

JEAN   Exactly! At the same time I was company
              secretary. So unless he was playing the
              Invisible Man that just isn't true.

CANTEL   (*very thoughtful*) Now why would he invent a
              thing like that?

              (ROSIE, *minus glasses, enters from hall.*)

ROSIE   Anyone seen my glasses?

JEAN   You were wearing them just now.

ROSIE   Not those. The others. Those are the pair I use
              for looking for the others and now I've lost
              those.

              (MRS PRATT, *in full cry, enters from hall, bears
              down on* CANTEL.)

MRS PRATT   Ah! I wish to see you. (*To* JEAN.) Young
              woman, I would be obliged if you would vacate
              my chair and leave the room.

JEAN   (*to* CANTEL) Don't worry about giving me that
              lift. I can easily walk to South Ken and take the
              tube.

CANTEL   (*nods*) See you later, dar . . . See you later.

              (JEAN *exits into hall.*)

MRS PRATT   Sit down.

CANTEL   Yes, sir!

MRS PRATT	Miss Lake, perhaps you may care to stay since it is your hotel which has been used as a brothel.
ROSIE	(*genuinely shocked*) Brothel? I hope Desiree didn't do it for money . . .
MRS PRATT	How dare you!
	(MARK *enters from hall, carrying a letter. He is followed in by* DOCTOR, *who is opening a letter, which he reads with quiet satisfaction.*)
MARK	The morning mail has at last arrived.
MRS PRATT	Ach!
	(MARK *hands* ROSIE *the letter which she opens. To* DOCTOR.) I wish to speak to you, too.
DOCTOR	We have nothing to discuss, Mrs Pratt.
ROSIE	(*looking myopically at letter*) Ho! It's Mrs Privett-Smith!
MRS PRATT	Dead?
ROSIE	No. (*Looks closer.*) Gone off, I think. Oh, bother it all! I can't read without my specs. (*Hands letter to* CANTEL.) Read it for me, love.
	(CANTEL *takes letter, looks at the end of it.*)
CANTEL	Yes, it's from Privett-Smith all right. (*Reads aloud.*) 'Dear Miss Lake, I have not said goodbye because you would have tried to persuade me that I am foolish to give up the comforts of the Delamere for the wilds of Canada . . .'
ROSIE	She's gone off to join her daughter! Oh! Thank heaven!
MRS PRATT	So much for your premonitions.
	(MARK *approaches* MRS PRATT *and speaks dramatically.*)

MARK   (*indicating* DOCTOR) And the sinister doctor
                breathes again! He hadn't wasted Mrs
                Privett-Smith after all! (*To* ROSIE.) In fact all we
                suspects can breathe again!

                (DOCTOR *smiles, folds his letter and exits into
                hall.*)

CANTEL   (*to* MARK) Do belt up. I haven't finished.
                (*Reads again.*) 'Poppy has always offered me a
                home in Canada and I suddenly decided to take
                her up on it. I telephoned her and she was
                thrilled'.

MRS PRATT   That is peculiar. They detest one another.

CANTEL   (*reading*) 'I am flying today, Saturday. I have
                left behind a few personal things. There is a
                powder compact which I know Lucy Fordyce
                always envied. I should like her to have it . . .'

ROSIE   What a shame! She would have loved it and
                now she's dead. Isn't that just like life?

CANTEL   (*reading*) 'I think that charming Squadron
                Leader might like the table lighter in the shape
                of a flying machine . . .' (*Shakes his head.*) I
                say that's rather touching.

MARK   (*apparently deeply moved*) Aaaah!

CANTEL   (*reading again*) 'The picture of the pussies in
                the leather frame is for you, dear Miss Lake'.

MARK   Aaaah!

ROSIE   How very kind! I've always hated that picture;
                but it's the thought that counts, isn't it?

CANTEL   (*reading*) 'Other friends may choose odd items
                that take their fancy. Affectionately yours,
                Muriel PS.'

MRS PRATT   I reserve the silver snuffbox.

ROSIE   I haven't seen a silver snuffbox.

MRS PRATT   She kept it hidden at the back of her wardrobe
               – ah – I think.

CANTEL   Just a sec. Mrs P S has written a PS. (*Reading.*)
               'PS: Nothing for Mrs Pratt and she knows why.
               Yours, Muriel P S.'

MRS PRATT   Typical spite! There's something strange about
               that letter. (*To* CANTEL.) Let me see it.
               (*Snatches it from him, eyes it closely.*) Hmm.
               Well, it *looks* like her writing.

ROSIE   It would, wouldn't it, if she wrote it?

MRS PRATT   If she wrote it. It strikes no one as peculiar that
               she should give this so-called gentleman a
               table lighter and refer to him as 'charming' a
               few days after calling him an ill-mannered
               bounder when he helped himself to all the
               mashed potatoes? The gift to him is completely
               out of character.

               (MRS PRATT *throws letter on to the side table
               with a triumphant gesture.* MARK *quietly and
               unseen picks it up and pockets it while* CANTEL
               is speaking.)

CANTEL   All right! I confess I forged that letter. I've
               always wanted that table lighter. I've lain
               awake nights plotting, planning how to get it . . .

ROSIE   (*slaps* CANTEL *with her fan*) Be quiet, you
               stupid boy! Oh, what a relief! Now all I have to
               worry about is my sanity!

               (MARK *moves towards hall door.*)

CANTEL   I want a word with you in private.

MARK   Not where I'm going. I'm funny that way.

               (MARK *exits into hall.* CANTEL *makes as if to
               follow him.*)

MRS PRATT   Just a moment, Squadron Leader Cantel.
               (CANTEL *pauses*.) You have behaved like an
               unmitigated cad and I shall claim substantial
               damages.

CANTEL   (*laughs*) Damages! What the hell did I damage?

ROSIE   Now, look, what's done is done . . .

MRS PRATT   It's easy for you to dismiss it, but he seduced
               my daughter.

CANTEL   *Once.*

MRS PRATT   Once was enough.

CANTEL   There we agree.

MRS PRATT   You see? And now he wants to cast her off like
               an old boot.

ROSIE   Look, love, are you complaining that he
               seduced her or isn't going on doing it?

MRS PRATT   Don't be flippant with me and don't call me
               'love'. Remember your place.

               (*Telephone rings.*)

ROSIE   Much more of that and I'll remember that your
               place is at your old table. (ROSIE *picks up
               telephone, puts on refined voice.*) Delamere
               Hotel . . . Speaking . . . What? . . . Speak up.
               It's a very bad line . . . Smith did you say? Do
               you want Mrs Privett-Smith or young Miss
               Jean Smith, who just . . . Mrs Privett-Smith?
               She's not here.

               (*During this* MARK *enters from hall and
               listens.*)

               What? Miss Privett-Smith? Sorry. She doesn't
               live here. She's in Canada. You what? You are
               Miss Privett-Smith? Poppy Privett-Smith! (*Cups
               phone, turns.*) It's Poppy Privett-Smith
               phoning from Canada! (*To phone again.*) And

how are you, love? And how is your dear
mother? Not too tired I hope. What? From her
journey . . . What? What! She flew to join you
. . . She told us in a letter I just received. I'll
read it to you. Hold on. (*Puts phone down,
turns to* CANTEL.) Where's that letter?

CANTEL   (*indicating* MRS PRATT) She has it.

MRS PRATT   I put it . . . (*Looks, reacts.*) It's gone!

ROSIE   Somebody must have it.

MRS PRATT   Wait a moment! (*To* MARK.) You picked it up.

MARK   That's right.

ROSIE   (*impatiently*) Give it, then, quick. This is
            costing the poor girl a fortune.

MARK   I haven't got it.

ROSIE   Then what have you done with it?

MARK   I threw it down the loo.

ROSIE   You've no business throwing other people's
            things down the loo.

MARK   Everybody had heard it and it didn't seem
            important.

ROSIE   Augh! (*Returns to phone.*) Hello? Miss
            Privett-Smith? I'm dreadfully sorry but the
            letter has been miss-looed-laid. It definitely
            said she was leaving to join you. Yes, give me
            your number. (*Scribbles number on a pad.*) Got
            it. I'm sure there will be some logical
            explanation . . . What! Never! Well, that's a
            horse of a different doo-dah. Yes, I think that
            would be your wisest course. (ROSIE, *looking
            extremely shaken, hangs up.*)Well!

MRS PRATT   Well?

ROSIE   Poppy Privett-Smith, by chance, had to call
            their bank in London this morning. The

Manager told her that her mother has been
steadily drawing out large sums in cash – up to
ten thousand pounds as of last Friday.

MRS PRATT   Smuggled it into Canada. Typical.

ROSIE   She never went to Canada!

                 (*General exclamations.*)

ALL   What?

ROSIE   Poppy didn't invite her. She said her mother
                 wouldn't fly, hated Canada and would never
                 have dreamed of going there.

MRS PRATT   Then we must seriously consider the question
                 – did she write that letter at all?

MARK   There you have a point.

CANTEL   (*to* MARK) And you conveniently got rid of it.

ROSIE   (*sagging*) And that knife's at my back again.

                 (*From offstage comes a somewhat eerie female
                 cry, causing all heads to turn.* DESIREE *enters
                 from hall, her face splattered with dirt, her
                 clothes soaked.*)

MRS PRATT   (*moves to her*) Look at you! What happened?

DESIREE   I fell in front of a bus.

ROSIE   It ran over you?

DESIREE   No. It swerved and hit a lamp post – but I
                 wanted it to hit me.

CANTEL   God!

MRS PRATT   How could you be such a fool? He's not worth it.

DESIREE   (*effort at control*) I'm sorry. Can somebody
                 please give me 10p?

CANTEL

(*eagerly*) Yes. Yes. Here you are.

(CANTEL *gives her 10p.* DESIREE *takes it, gives him a long look, then turns and exits into hall.*)

What does she want 10p for?

ROSIE

Only the gas meter in her room. THE GAS METER! No!

(MRS PRATT, CANTEL *and* MARK *hurry from the room.* ROSIE *starts to follow but stops, calls out.*)

No! It's all right. We're converted to North Sea and you can't kill yourself with that. Oh! I can't stand much more of this.

(*She goes to bottle but it's empty. Then she has a sudden idea. She glances up passage, hurries to alcove, draws aside curtain and looks at trunk, makes her mind up and goes inside. The curtains fall again hiding her.* DOCTOR *enters from hall. He is carrying the kukri in his hand. He looks over his shoulder, quickly pulls door almost shut, then advances silently on the alcove, knife in hand. He draws back one curtain to reveal* ROSIE *with her back to him. She turns and utters a blood-curdling scream. She clutches at his upraised arm and screams again. He puts a hand over her mouth.*)

DOCTOR

No! No please . . .

ROSIE

Get away! Get away from me!

DOCTOR

Please, I. . .

(MARK *hurries in from hall.*)

MARK

What the . . . ? (DOCTOR *hastily releases* ROSIE *who staggers away.*) What's happening here?

ROSIE (*gasping*) I was going to look in the trunk. He came at me . . . from behind . . . knife . . .

DOCTOR No! No! I was going to look into trunk, too.

MARK Why the knife, doctor?

DOCTOR To force lock if necessary.

MARK I thought Cantel indicated it was unlocked. Let's all have a look, shall we? (MARK *approaches trunk, flips the lock which is unlocked. He opens trunk.* ROSIE *and* DOCTOR *both move in.*) Flying suit, books, silver cups. No body.

MARK (*lowers lid*) Satisfied?

DOCTOR I am sorry. I . . . I am very, very sorry.

  (DOCTOR, *looking beside himself with mortification, exits into hall.* ROSIE *staggers to bottle, again registers it's empty.*)

MARK You really think he was after you, Rosie?

ROSIE Yes. No. Oh, I don't know. I don't know anything any more. I just saw the knife and remembered Tim's warning. Excuse me. (*Waves bottle.*) Going to pop down to the cellar.

MARK Don't stay down too long.

  (ROSIE *exits into hall.* MARK *walks to alcove, closes curtains, comes back thoughtfully.* CANTEL *enters from hall.*)

CANTEL What's up with Rosie?

MARK Imagination running riot again. How's Desiree?

CANTEL All right. Not contemplating anything stupid. (*He goes to phone and dials.*) Police, please. (*Intercepts a look from* MARK.) Somebody has to do it. That call from Canada was not Rosie's imagination. (MARK *nods*.) Don't look so worried. You have plenty of time to rustle up an excuse for destroying that letter.

MARK I have. I was in a rage because she didn't leave me a table lighter.

CANTEL What was the idea in putting me down to that new girl?

MARK Jean Smith? I didn't put you down; just gave her a rundown on the inmates, you included.

CANTEL That's not what it sounded like to me.

MARK How would you know about my talk with her, anyway?

CANTEL (*waves a hand at* MARK, *talks to phone*) Hullo? Police? I'm speaking from the Delamere Hotel, 27 Queen's Gate Grove, SW7. A lady resident has disappeared under somewhat suspicious circumstances. Thank you. The name is Cantel. Squadron Leader Cantel. (*Hangs up.*) They're sending someone. (*Moves down to stand near* MARK.) I assume you can also give them a good reason for lying about being an actor at Worthing last summer? (MARK *gives a slight reaction, but says nothing.*) No hot denials? Interesting! What exactly are you?

MARK An actor who *didn't* appear at Worthing last summer.

CANTEL But why the lies?

MARK One gets a little shame-faced about being permanently out of work.

CANTEL A very broke actor, huh?

MARK That you can say again.

CANTEL   I would if you hadn't got a hefty wad of notes
          hidden at the back of your sock drawer
          upstairs.

          (MARK *looks at him hard, then smiles, shakes
          his head and produces a door key.*)

MARK   My room is locked.

          (CANTEL *grins and produces a similar key.*)

CANTEL   We all know Rosie's problem is losing keys.
          What *you* don't know is that she partially
          solved it by having all the bedroom locks the
          same.

MARK   And what the hell gives you the right to nose
          around my room?

CANTEL   I suddenly got to be terribly interested in you.
          By the way, Rosie has been sounding off about
          some cash she thinks is missing from Lucy
          Fordyce's room.

MARK   That's hardly proof I nicked it.

CANTEL   No, but questions breed questions, don't they?
          The money, the lies about Worthing, then the
          Privett-Smith letter. If it was a forgery who
          would want to destroy it, once that call from
          Canada let the cat out of the bag? Answer, the
          forger. Who did destroy it? You.

MARK   And are you planning to air these theories to
          the police?

CANTEL   Can you give me any reason why I shouldn't?

MARK   Let me try, Squadron Leader. But what am I
          saying! It isn't Squadron Leader, is it Squadron
          Leader? It was Flight Sergeant wasn't it,
          Squadron Leader? Flight Sergeant
          dishonourably discharged to boot; in fact,
          booted out lock stock and stripes. (CANTEL

has gone very still.) No hot denials?
Interesting!

CANTEL   How . . . How did you . . . ?

MARK   Sheer luck. I met a guy who was actually in
           your squadron. It was silly of you to give the
           real number.

CANTEL   (*regaining confidence*) So I added a few rings
           I'm not entitled to and kept quiet about a piece
           of foolishness. Not much harm in that is there?

MARK   But does it provide a basis on which we might
           sign a mutual non-aggression pact?

           (CANTEL *hesitates then gives a brief nod.*)

CANTEL   Yes, but not for the reasons you may suppose.

MARK   I know the reason – Jean Smith.

CANTEL   (*shaken*) How the hell . . . ?

MARK   Rosie caught you snogging and she can never
           keep her mouth shut. You have good taste.

CANTEL   We're getting married tomorrow. She has a
           somewhat influential father, who doesn't know
           of my existence. I want to keep it that way until
           it's too late for him to screw things up.

MARK   (*sticks out his hand*) And the best of luck,
           sarge; or dare I say partner?

           (CANTEL *ignores his hand, eyes him curiously.*)

CANTEL   Did you have anything to do with mother
           Privett-Smith's disappearance?

MARK   I'd be rather rash to make any statement in the
           absence of a corpse, wouldn't I?

(*Offstage comes a series of blood-curdling screams* (ROSIE.) *She staggers in from hall, an unopened bottle of whisky in one hand. She is beside herself.*)

ROSIE   Oh! Oh! She's in the cellar! On the floor! Stretched out. Stiff as a poker. Dead!

(*Blackout.*)

ACT TWO

Time: Monday 8.30 pm.

*As the lights rise the stage is empty. The curtains have been
drawn across the window bay. The curtains are now also
closed over the alcove. The fire is alight.*

MRS PRATT   (*offstage*) Disgusting food. For the pigs.

                 (MRS PRATT *enters from dining room wearing a
                 formidable evening creation. She is followed
                 by* DESIREE, *who had also changed into
                 another disaster.*)

                 That chef has gone completely to pot, but I
                 suppose that is to be expected when a
                 Chinaman has the gall to attempt Irish Stew.

DESIREE   Can you wonder? Everyone is at sixes and
                 sevens.

                 (MRS PRATT *has moved to the hall door which
                 is ajar. She peeps out into hall. Sound of*
                 MARK *and another man talking offstage.*)

MRS PRATT   Good gracious! That policeman is still making
                 gruff noises at young Anderson. No doubt
                 putting some searching questions about his
                 destruction of that letter, as well he should . . .
                 (*Sits in her chair.*) And it's disgraceful
                 sending a mere sergeant to investigate a
                 murder.

DESIREE   We still don't know it's murder.

MRS PRATT   Of course it is, and he lets your precious
                 Squadron Leader walk out scot free.

DESIREE   Mumsie, I know how you feel about Tim. All
                 right, he is a so-and-so, but why on earth
                 would he want to kill Mrs Privett-Smith?

MRS PRATT   For ten thousand pounds *cash*.

DESIREE   That's ridiculous. He's just landed a super new
                 job abroad.

MRS PRATT   Muriel Privett-Smith left the hotel on Saturday
                 morning presumably with the money. He left
                 just after she did. Late last night he sneaks
                 back here with that trunk, is surprised by Miss
                 Lake, who says the trunk was obviously heavy.

DESIREE   Honestly. He used it to bring back his gear
                 from the flying club.

MRS PRATT   That huge trunk for a few paperbacks and a
                 couple of swimming cups? (*Rises, beckons and
                 moves towards alcove.*) Come here. Look
                 inside.

DESIREE   We can't.

MRS PRATT   Yes, we can. It's unlocked. I've already looked.
                 (DESIREE *makes a helpless gesture.*) I am
                 convinced that last night this trunk contained a
                 body. See? Plenty of room.

                 (*So saying,* MRS PRATT *throws open the lid of
                 the trunk. With startling effect. Hopefully both
                 to the audience, as well as to* MRS PRATT *and*
                 DESIREE, *a man's figure shoots up out of the
                 trunk like some scary jack-in-the-box. It is the*
                 DOCTOR. DESIREE *screams.* MRS PRATT *gasps and
                 clutches her heart.* DOCTOR *is seen to have
                 something in his hand which he endeavours to
                 conceal.*)

DOCTOR   I am sorry. Excuse me, please.

                 (DOCTOR *pockets the object in his hand. We see
                 a flash of metal. He steps out of the trunk and
                 moves quickly towards the hall door.* MRS
                 PRATT *recovers full volume.*)

MRS PRATT   Just one moment, Doctor Ali. (DOCTOR
             pauses.) I demand to know what you were
             doing in that trunk?

DOCTOR   I – uh – it was Yoga. A Yoga exercise.

             (DOCTOR *exits hurriedly into hall*.)

MRS PRATT   Yoga my foot! Either he is insane, or is up to
             no good. He had something in his hand.

DESIREE   Yes. It was metal . . .

MRS PRATT   A knife! He was holding a knife again. He and
             Cantel must be in league.

DESIREE   Mummy you're not seriously suggesting that
             Tim killed Mrs Privett-Smith and put her in this
             trunk?

MRS PRATT   I'm not suggesting. I am sure of it.

DESIREE   (*accusing*) But why would he bring the body
             back *here*?

             (MRS PRATT *looks a bit floored by this one but
             makes a good recovery*.)

MRS PRATT   I am not paid to answer stupid questions.

DESIREE   Anyway, Rosie met him when he came in and
             she said he was perfectly normal.

MRS PRATT   More than she is. Mad as a hatter.

DESIREE   Give her a chance! She was dreadfully upset
             after that awful shock in the cellar.

MRS PRATT   Obviously. Her screams must have been
             audible for miles.

DESIREE   She loved that cat of hers. Seeing it lying there
             dead. Poor little Raggles.

             (ROSIE *enters from hall dressed entirely in
             black even to a pair of black spectacles and a
             black fan*.)

MRS PRATT   Good heavens! Look at you! Was it really
             necessary to go into full mourning?

ROSIE   Raggles was very dear to me.

DESIREE   Try not to brood about it, Rosie, dear.

ROSIE   How can one help being broody . . . ? (ROSIE'S
             hand pats DESIREE'S *stomach. She withdraws it
             quickly.*) Sorry, love. Nothing intended.

MRS PRATT   We, have more important matters to discuss
             than the death of your mangy old cat in the
             cellar.

ROSIE   Mangy! I'll swing for you . . .

             (ROSIE *makes a move towards* MRS PRATT *but*
             DESIREE *holds her back with a calming
             gesture. Unmoved,* MRS PRATT *moves to the hall
             door and peeks out.*)

MRS PRATT   I don't believe it. That Sergeant is still with
             Anderson. What *are* they talking about?

ROSIE   (*grandly*) I am not in the habit of
             eavesdropping, Mrs Potter.

             (*Despite this,* ROSIE *goes to door, edges* MRS
             PRATT *aside and peeks out herself.*)

MRS PRATT   No doubt . . .

ROSIE   (*waving her down*) Tsst! I'm eavesdropping.
             (ROSIE *listens hard.*) No, can't hear a thing.
             (*Moves away from door.*) I wonder why Mark
             Anderson destroyed that letter? Most peculiar.

MRS PRATT   Very prudent – if he forged it.

DESIREE   Not him, too! Two minutes ago you were
             accusing Tim Cantel of killing Mrs
             Privett-Smith, and no one knows if she's even
             dead. Honestly!

MRS PRATT   (*ignoring* DESIREE) They could all be in it
             together.

ROSIE   All?

MRS PRATT   Anderson, Cantel and the doctor.

ROSIE   What makes you suspect the doctor?

MRS PRATT   He is full of surprises your charming Oriental.
             Do you know what we just caught him doing?

ROSIE   I don't want to know if it's something rude.

MRS PRATT   He was hiding in that trunk.

             (ROSIE *is definitely surprised. She looks
             towards* DESIREE *for confirmation.* DESIREE
             nods.)

ROSIE   *Inside* it?

MRS PRATT   With the lid closed.

ROSIE   He has some very funny ways.

MRS PRATT   I opened the lid and he shot out like some
             fearful jack-in-the-box brandishing a knife.

ROSIE   Again! Go on!

DESIREE   We can't be sure it was a knife, Mumsie, and
             he wasn't brandishing it, whatever it was.

MRS PRATT   Oh, be quiet! (*To* ROSIE.) He owed you money, yes?

ROSIE   And paid me this morning.

MRS PRATT   But where, I wonder, did he manage to find the
             money?

ROSIE   He said it had just arrived.

MRS PRATT   Lies! The post did not come until lunchtime,
             after he had paid you!

ROSIE	(*despite herself*) Yes! I never thought of that.
MRS PRATT	And what about his row with Mrs Privett-Smith on Thursday night? What about his threat that I would suffer the same fate as she?
ROSIE	And the key – and that knife in my back . . . But the *three* of them in cahoots? That's stretching it a bit.
MRS PRATT	All three of them were away on Saturday night.
ROSIE	That's right! They were.
MRS PRATT	Somewhere together, and . . .
ROSIE	Tsst! Shut up! Shut up!
MRS PRATT	I beg your pardon?
ROSIE	I'm thinking.
	(ROSIE *helps herself to a drink.*)
MRS PRATT	That is no cause to be ill-mannered.
ROSIE	Sorry, but I'm better equipped to deal with this than you are.
MRS PRATT	(*bridling*) Why? It's *my* theory.
ROSIE	I played the role often enough, didn't I?
MRS PRATT	Role? What role?
ROSIE	You know, the Agatha Thingy detective woman. Whatsername. Sharples. Ena Sharples.
DESIREE	Marple.
ROSIE	That's it. When you've played a character often enough you get right inside it and start thinking like it. That's what I did with Miss Marbles. During the run of this particular play 'Murder At The Thingummy', I think it was, we had a whatsomaniac in the cast.
MRS PRATT	(*with meaning*) Dipsomaniac?

ROSIE	No, the one that steals things like Miss Daintee. Insomniac . . . no . . .
DESIREE	Kleptomaniac.
ROSIE	That's it. Meptoklaniac. Anyway, the police were called in and were completely baffled. (*To* MRS PRATT.) Guess who spotted the thief. Go on. Guess.
MRS PRATT	(*turning away*.) No, I shan't.
ROSIE	You've guessed. Yes, me! I worked it out entirely on my own, by assembling the facts, then fitting them together. Now, let's see what we have . . .
MRS PRATT	A treble scotch by the look of it. I thought you only drank at weekends.
ROSIE	(*pacing*) I'm making this an exception. Now, what have we got? Fact – the doctor definitely had a row with Muriel Privett-Hedge. Fact – the doctor tells Mrs Pitt . . .
MRS PRATT	Pratt!
ROSIE	. . . that Muriel's disappearance had something to do with that row. Fact – the doctor threatens Mrs Potts . . .
MRS PRATT	Pratt!
ROSIE	. . . with the same fate. Fact –
MRS PRATT	And stop saying 'fact'.
ROSIE	And you stop saying Pratt. Fact – Muriel Thing draws out ten thousand pounds from the bank and disappears. A letter, forged, says she's gone to Canada. Fact – the Squadron Leader arrives back late last night with that trunk, which contains nothing suspicious when

examined by the police today. Those are the facts. Now, assumptions.

(ROSIE *takes a swig.*)

MRS PRATT   *Consumptions.*

ROSIE   Muriel Privett-Thing is meeting these three, by prior arrangement. Why?

MRS PRATT   Because . . .

ROSIE   Shut up! She's been lured by some get-rich-quick scheme and they meet at a secret rendezvous. (*Ponders.*) Where?

MRS PRATT   (*loudly*) Marylebone High Street.

ROSIE   What a daft idea. Who ever heard of a secret assignation in a High Street? And why Marylebone? Why not Kensington . . .

MRS PRATT   Because Miss Tipples . . .

ROSIE   Sharples.

DESIREE   Marple.

MRS PRATT   Marylebone High Street is where that shifty doctor carries out illegal operations.

ROSIE   Get away?

MRS PRATT   You don't know everything, you see? Muriel Privett-Smith caught him coming out of a house there several times. And this is another reason why he should wish to rub her out.

DESIREE   Rub her out! You sound like Humphrey Bogart.

ROSIE   (*warming to this*) It's a possibility. It fits. A doctor's undercover surgery. Oodles of drugs to hand – some of them lethal. Curare, strychnine, prussic acid, cyanide. (*Aside.*) That's the one with the distinctive odour of bitter lemon.

MRS PRATT	(*derisive*) Bitter lemon! It's burned almonds.
DESIREE	Bitter almonds actually, Mumsie.
MRS PRATT	Stop interfering. Go and watch television or something.
ROSIE	Or perhaps he used some unknown Hindu drug.
MRS PRATT	He's a Pakistani.
ROSIE	He could still use a Hindu drug.
DESIREE	But Muslims don't like Hindus.
ROSIE	Alright then, a Muslin drug, something unknown to the Western World. Under some pretext she is given an injection. (*Starts to act it all dramatically.*) She goes rigid. (*Aside.*) It acts very fast. She chokes. She clutches her throat, her eyes bulge from their sockets, her legs give way and she collapses to the ground. We hear the horrible sound of the death rattle. (*Gives a death rattle.*) Silence. She is dead.
MRS PRATT	Why would they go to all that trouble? Three strong men. They'd only need thump her on the head with a blunt instrument.
ROSIE	She would fight like a tigress.
MRS PRATT	At 68, six stone and five foot two?
ROSIE	Have you ever seen a bantam-weight in action? They pick up the body and dump it in that trunk.
DESIREE	Then bring it back here! As I said to Mumsie, that's a crazy idea.
ROSIE	Not at all. If you study the criminal mentality it makes perfect sense.
DESIREE	How?

ROSIE   (*triumphant*) Because this is the *last* place the
                 police would dream of looking. Yes, it all
                 begins to fit together like some macabre jigsaw
                 puzzle. They have just taken the body out
                 when I surprise them. They cosh me.
                 Aaaaaagh! I fall. Then what . . . ?

MRS PRATT   They could have stuffed her up in the attic.

ROSIE   (*reacts*) They *what?* Oh, I see what you mean.

MRS PRATT   Or bricked her up in the cellar.

ROSIE   No. I doubt that. I've been . . . I think I'd have
                 noticed anything odd in the cellar.

DESIREE   Really! You two! There's only one thing
                 missing, besides a body.

ROSIE   What?

DESIREE   The butler.

ROSIE   Butler?

DESIREE   Don't you remember? It's always the butler
                 who turns out to have done it in the end. You
                 are a pair! You sit there, stirring it up, stirring,
                 stirring . . .

                 (*Almost suffocating with laughter, and talking
                 as she goes,* DESIREE *exits into hall.*)

ROSIE   Do you think being pregnant's made her funny
                 in the head?

MRS PRATT   She was always simple. We had a very clumsy
                 nurse who kept dropping her.

ROSIE   Hello! That policeman's leaving at last. Ooh!
                 He's taking Mark Anderson with him.

                 (ROSIE *remains by hall door.* MRS PRATT *moves
                 to window, draws back lace curtain. It is dark
                 outside.*)

MRS PRATT   Is he in handcuffs?

ROSIE   No, but that doesn't mean he's off the hook.
                 This is what's called 'helping the police with
                 their enquiries'.

MRS PRATT   (*nods*) Which means being locked in a
                 soundproof cell and bludgeoned with rubber
                 truncheons.

ROSIE   (*admiringly*) I didn't know you were into all this.

MRS PRATT   I keep my ear to the ground.

ROSIE   We could make quite a partnership! Oh, by the
                 way, to give him his due, it wasn't the doctor
                 who stole Lucy Fordyce's little hoard.

MRS PRATT   Let me guess – it was Cantel.

ROSIE   No. Me. Clean forgot I'd picked it up and put it
                 away in the laundry basket.

MRS PRATT   Well, the doctor would hardly be interested in
                 Miss Fordyce's pathetic little hoard when he's
                 in on a three-way split with Cantel and
                 Anderson with the ten big ones.

ROSIE   Quick! The doctor is coming. Sit down. Act
                 nonchalant. Let me handle this.

MRS PRATT   Handle what?

ROSIE   A little discreet interrogation.

MRS PRATT   He's no fool. He's wily. All Orientals are.

ROSIE   Leave it to me. He won't notice a thing. It's a
                 technique. Watch it.

                 (ROSIE *drapes herself on sofa.* DOCTOR *enters
                 from hall.*)

ROSIE   (*over-joyful*) Doctor, dear! What a delightful
               surprise! Will you join me in a drink?

               (ROSIE *rises, goes to him sinuously.*)

DOCTOR   Thank you, no. I never drink, as you will
               remember.

ROSIE   Of course! That's why you look so healthy. All
               that yogurt and Yoga. I am right, you do
               practise Yoga, don't you?

DOCTOR   (*straight off*) You are trying to find out what I
               am doing in that trunk, isn't it?

ROSIE   No! You do anything you like in the trunk. Feel
               at home. Ha! Ha!

               (DOCTOR *locates his Urdu newspaper, which is
               on the sofa table, picks it up.*)

               By the way, I hope I thanked you properly for
               paying me this morning.

DOCTOR   Why do you thank me for paying what I owe?

ROSIE   (*very casual*) You said, 'It came by post this
               morning'.

DOCTOR   No. I am receiving a, letter this morning but I
               am paying you before post arrived, as you will
               remember

ROSIE   Did you? So you did! Ha! Ha! I'll be forgetting
               my own name next.

DOCTOR   The letter you saw me open was from hospital
               Informing me that I have MRCP.

ROSIE   (*concerned*) Oh? I hope it's nothing catching.

               (MRS PRATT'S *eyes go skywards.*)

DOCTOR   (*patiently*) No, Miss Lake. MRCP. What I have
           been studying for. Member of the College of
           Physicians.

ROSIE   Oh! Ah! Yes! Member of the Royal thing . . .
           thing . . . Congratulations. So your course is
           over, of course?

DOCTOR   Yes.

ROSIE   (*very offhand*) No more toiling off to
           Marylebone High Street.

DOCTOR   My course was in Ducane Road, Hammersmith,
           you remember.

ROSIE   Silly me! I must have been muddled.

DOCTOR   Or misled, Miss Lake. Excuse me, please.

ROSIE   I wonder what on earth made me mention
           Marylebone High Street?

           (DOCTOR *has moved up to hall door, where he
           turns. His voice takes on a steely quality as it
           has done before.*)

DOCTOR   Either Mrs Privett-Smith or this woman here
           will have told you.

MRS PRATT Don't you call me a woman, my man.

DOCTOR   (*ignoring* MRS PRATT) Miss Lake, I am valuing
           your good opinion of me, therefore I tell you
           that I visit number 412 Marylebone High Street
           to see the girl I hope to marry. Her name is
           Saida Khan. I have already told this to the
           Police Officer who is wishing me to account for
           movements on Saturday night. I was with her.
           She loaned me the money, by the way.

ROSIE   Congratulations again. Isn't that romantic!

DOCTOR   As to trunk I will explain later when we are alone.

           (DOCTOR *exits into hall.*)

MRS PRATT   Discreet interrogation! A fine hash you made
             of that!

ROSIE   I did! It was your fault.

MRS PRATT   (*rising*) My fault?

ROSIE   Illegal operations! He's as innocent as a
             newborn babe, you stupid old fool.

MRS PRATT   (*advancing*) I will not be spoken to like that by
             a common hotelier.

ROSIE   Common . . . I may be common but I'm not an
             evil-tongued old bitch.

MRS PRATT   Augh!

             (MRS PRATT *lams out with her cane and catches*
             ROSIE *a good one round her buttocks*.)

ROSIE   Why you . . .

             (ROSIE *raises her closed fan and clocks* MRS
             PRATT *sharply on the top of her head*.)

MRS PRATT   Aaaaah!

             (MRS PRATT *goes rigid, makes strangled noises
             reminiscent of* ROSIE'S *imitation of the
             drugging of Mrs Privett-Smith*. MRS PRATT
             *staggers into the alcove, collides with the
             trunk and collapses beside it. She lies still –
             very still, perhaps half concealed behind
             trunk*.)

ROSIE   (*unimpressed*) And that was a rotten fall. Come
             on! You're not kidding anyone, you know.
             (MRS PRATT *does not move*.) Come on, this is
             not the last act of Hamlet. (MRS PRATT *does not
             move*.) You can stay there 'till the cows come
             home, love. I don't care. I'm off. Ta-ta!

(ROSIE *moves to dining room door.* MRS PRATT
does not move. ROSIE *shows the first signs of
anxiety and returns to her side, tickles her.*)
Tickle, tickle, tickle. I'm going this time. I really
am. Bye bye! (ROSIE *clumps noisily off towards
hall then closes hall door loudly but remains
inside the room.* MRS PRATT *does not move.*
ROSIE *begins really to panic at last. She
hurries back to alcove.*) Get up! Stop playing
silly games! (MRS PRATT *does not move.* ROSIE
*kneels down. She pats her cheek. She bends
closer to listen for breathing. Utter horror
now shows on her face. She gasps audibly as
hall door opens and* DOCTOR *enters again.*)

DOCTOR There is another . . . (*Sees* MRS PRATT.) What
has happened?

ROSIE (*incoherent*) She . . . I . . . fell. She doesn't
seem to be . . .

(DOCTOR *hurries to* MRS PRATT *and kneels
down.*)

DOCTOR She has probably fainted. Always she is eating
too much, too fast.

(DOCTOR *picks up* MRS PRATT'S *wrist to take her
pulse. Both he and* ROSIE *freeze as* MISS
DAINTEE *enters from dining room, smiles at*
ROSIE, *looks towards the strange tableau made
by* DOCTOR *and* MRS PRATT, *waves amiably
towards them and exits into hall.*)

DOCTOR I am sorry, Miss Lake. She is dead.

ROSIE (*faintly*) Dead!

(ROSIE *sways faintly.* DOCTOR *moves and
supports her.*)

DOCTOR Probably a massive coronary.

ROSIE No. I killed her.

DOCTOR You must not say foolish things.

ROSIE   But I did. She hit me and I hit her back.

DOCTOR   You hit her on the back?

ROSIE   No, on the head, the top of her head.

DOCTOR   (*frowns*) With what?

ROSIE   (*showing closed fan*) This.

DOCTOR   Miss Lake! This fan could not crack an egg.
               (DOCTOR *takes fan and deals himself a sharp
               blow on the head with it.*) You see? This could
               not kill her.

ROSIE   (*stubbornly*) It did. Look. there she is, large as
               life – dead.

DOCTOR   But it could not unless she is one of these
               people who are born with skull like eggshell.
               (*Thoughtfully.*) This is, of course, just
               possible. (*Moves back towards* MRS PRATT.) If
               she had some rare condition like I am saying
               then you cannot blame yourself.

ROSIE   But I do. I'm a murderer. I'll hang. No I won't.
               it's life imprisonment and that's worse. We're
               ever such a long-lived family.

DOCTOR   (*thinks hard*) That old woman, Miss Daintee,
               she has seen us. Will she talk?

ROSIE   No! Even if she noticed anything she'll forget
               all about it. She sometimes has three meals one
               after the other and then thinks she hasn't
               eaten. Why?

DOCTOR   You should not be punished or suffer for this
               in any way. Perhaps we can avoid this.

ROSIE   I can't bribe my way out of trouble here. This is
               England not Pakiwhatsit.

DOCTOR | I am saying nobody is needing to know you have anything to do with it. We take her up to her room.

ROSIE | (*befuddled*) How does that help? I'll have to let the room sometime. She's bound to be found eventually.

DOCTOR | (*patiently*) She will be alone in her room and it will look as if she had a fall.

ROSIE | But why should you risk . . . ?

DOCTOR | Because you always have been too good to me, my friend.

ROSIE | I don't like it. Your career could be ruined.

DOCTOR | No problem. We carry her up in the Squadron Leader's trunk.

ROSIE | Oh! Now I'm a trunk murderer.

DOCTOR | Like this no one is suspicious even if we meet people on the way. Where is Squadron Leader?

ROSIE | He went out about fifteen minutes ago. The policeman said everyone was free to come and go.

DOCTOR | Good. Come. You must help me. (ROSIE *and* DOCTOR *go through curtains into alcove.*) Make sure curtains are closed. (ROSIE *completely closes the curtains, hiding them from view.*) Now take her legs. (*Sound of movement and exertion.*)

ROSIE | (*off*) Poor Mrs Pratt! How often have I said I could kill her . . . May I be forgiven.

DOCTOR | (*off*) Careful now. That is the way.

ROSIE | (*off*) And Desiree. What's to become of her?

DOCTOR | (*off*) I think now she will have the chance to live a much better life.

ROSIE   (*off*) Shut the lid.

             (DOCTOR *and* ROSIE *reappear through the*
             curtains. DOCTOR *moves to hall door, looks out*
             in both directions. He comes back again,
             shaking his head.)

DOCTOR   We must wait. Miss Daintee is sitting on the
             stairs, eating.

ROSIE   Ach! She may even go to sleep there. I need a
             drink. (*Moves to sideboard.*) You, doctor?

DOCTOR   No, thank you. I never drink as you will
             remember.

             (ROSIE *pours a hefty drink.*)

ROSIE   I don't know how you keep so calm. Hiding
             bodies in trunks.

DOCTOR   To me death is no stranger.

ROSIE   Yes, I suppose it wouldn't be. (*Hint of*
             suspicion.) But . . . not . . . in trunks, like this?

DOCTOR   (*smiles*) No!

ROSIE   (*after a mental struggle*) Doctor, you said
             you'd tell me. What were you doing hiding in
             that trunk?

DOCTOR   (*smiles again*) I am wanting to examine
             something quietly. This time I wait until people
             are eating. It is easier if I stand inside. Then
             Mrs Pratt and daughter come out too soon. I do
             not want to be seen so I sit down and close lid.
             Then Mrs Pratt opens lid and finds me.

ROSIE   But why come out brandishing that knife
             again?

DOCTOR   It was not a knife. (*Produces a magnifying glass.*) Magnifying glass to look for traces of blood.

ROSIE   Blood! Then *you* believe Mrs Privett-Smith's body *was* in there . . . ?

DOCTOR   No, I think it was not. I am examining to make sure. Squadron Leader is not a murderer. You see, Mrs Privett-Smith is alive.

ROSIE   You *know* that?

DOCTOR   (*nods*) I am having this quarrel with her on Thursday. She is another with a bad tongue. I have a strong solicitor's letter sent to her threatening sewage for defamation of character. This letter arrived here on Saturday morning. I think it scared her. She panicked, packed bags and ran away.

ROSIE   But the forged letter about Canada . . .

DOCTOR   Not forged. She wrote it herself to hide tracks. As Mr Anderson says, you probably are finding her in Bournemouth with Colonel Forbes.

ROSIE   Oh, that's wonderful! I can breathe again. There's been no murder! (*Reacts.*) Yes, there has! I've done one. I can't stand it! Every time I get out of one hole I fall into another.

DOCTOR   Look into hall. See if we can move now.

                (DOCTOR *enters alcove, disappears.* ROSIE *opens hall door as* CANTEL *marches in, scaring the daylights out of her.*)

ROSIE   Aaaaagh! (*Loudly to* DOCTOR.) Squadron Leader! It's the *Squadron Leader!* (*Seizes him, swings him round so his back is to alcove.*) Gorgeous beast! Incredible bulk! Oh, if I was a few years younger . . .

CANTEL   You're joking. I'm yours here and now for a packet of crisps. (*Lowers voice.*) What's happened to Mrs Pratt?

ROSIE   (*loud*) What do you mean?

CANTEL   Where are she and Desiree?

ROSIE   Oh! Ah! Yes! Desiree's upstairs and you must have run into Mrs Pratt.

CANTEL   When?

ROSIE   Now. This minute. She went out just as you came in.

CANTEL   Missed her, thank God! (*Sudden thought.*) Damn! I knew I'd forgotten something.

ROSIE   What?

CANTEL   I've run out of vodka. Meant to buy a bottle while I was out. Do you have one by any chance?

ROSIE   Sorry, love, I don't . . . YES! There's a whole case in the cellar.

CANTEL   Mind it I nick one? I'll replace it tomorrow.

ROSIE   (*delighted, relieved*) Go down and help yourself. Take two! Three! By the way, it may be a bit hard to find. It's behind some crates of wine.

          (CANTEL *pecks her on the cheek and exits into hall.*)

ROSIE   (*goes to door, peeks out*) He's gone.

          (DOCTOR *opens curtains.*)

DOCTOR   You did well.

ROSIE   Better than you think. He could be down there hours. There's no vodka in the cellar.

DOCTOR	Quick then, We go now.
	(DOCTOR's *head disappears behind the curtains.* ROSIE *turns away from hall door.* DESIREE *enters behind her.*)
DESIREE	(*loudly*) Mumsie!
ROSIE	(*a yell*) AAAAGH!
DESIREE	What . . . ?
ROSIE	(*seizing her*) Desiree! How pretty you look! *Gorgeous!* What have you done to yourself?
DESIREE	Nothing. (*Looks closer.*) Are you feeling all right?
ROSIE	Wonderful, but you look *dreadful.*
DESIREE	You just said I looked gorgeous!
ROSIE	I made a mistake. A trick of the light. Go to bed.
DESIREE	Have you seen Mummy?
ROSIE	No.
DESIREE	She was here.
ROSIE	Yes.
DESIREE	Then where did she go?
ROSIE	Out.
DESIREE	Out? In this weather? It's drizzling.
ROSIE	Out of the room.
DESIREE	Yes, but where? She isn't in her bedroom or the telly room. BBC 2 is showing a film she wanted to see, *Mummy's Coffin.*
ROSIE	(*groans*) Aaah!
DESIREE	Are you okay? (ROSIE *gulps, nods.*) So where is she?

ROSIE   The cellar!

DESIREE   The cellar?

ROSIE   Your mother's in the cellar with the
                 Scoutmaster . . . Squadron Leader.

DESIREE   But she's never been to the cellar in her life.

ROSIE   That's just what she said, 'Rosie', she said.
                 'Do you know', she said, 'I've never been to
                 the cellar in all these years'. She said.

DESIREE   So what?

ROSIE   So she went, with him.

DESIREE   But why?

ROSIE   He was looking for vodka and she was looking
                 for – um . . . clues. Yes, clues.

DESIREE   About your cat?

ROSIE   No. Mrs Privett-Whatsit. You remember we
                 were saying she might be bricked down up
                 there? I mean up, down there.

DESIREE   Oh, gosh! She could have tripped down those
                 steps and cracked her skull.

ROSIE   Aaaah! No, no. I don't think that's very likely.
                 Impossible, in fact.

DESIREE   Tch! I'd better get down there. I wish you two
                 would stop playing amateur detectives.

                 (DESIREE *exits into hall.* DOCTOR *emerges
                 through curtains.*)

DOCTOR   Keep calm, Miss Lake. The worst is over.

ROSIE   (*all in*) It had better be or you'll have another
                 corpse on your hands. (DOCTOR *starts to move*

*towards hall door to make sure the coast is
clear.* ROSIE *sees* MRS PRATT'S *fur sticking out
of the trunk and lets out a muted scream which
brings the* DOCTOR *to a halt.*) Look! Her fur!
You've left her fur hanging out.

(ROSIE *hastens back to trunk and flips open
the clasp. She raises the lid, leaves it open
and starts hastily to bundle the fur back
inside.* DOCTOR *hurries back into alcove.*
ROSIE'S *back is to audience as she kneels
before the trunk. Her hands will therefore be
invisible. NB: it has been found useful to have
a dummy representing* MRS PRATT *inside the
trunk.*)

Hold the lid.

(DESIREE *enters from the hall.*)

DESIREE   I say!

(DESIREE'S *arrival has a catastrophic effect on*
ROSIE *and* DOCTOR. *In a reflex action the*
DOCTOR *slams the lid of the trunk shut, not
realising that one or both of* ROSIE'S *hands are
still inside.* ROSIE *gives a loud yell, jumps up,
then dances round the room wringing her
hands and uttering strange Indian war dance
noises.*)

ROSIE   Oh-Aaaah-Eeeeee-Wooooo-Ow-Owa! Whew!

(DESIREE *stands with hands on hips watching
this.* DOCTOR *moves to stand in front of the
trunk.*)

DESIREE   That'll teach you – getting up to no good.

DOCTOR   H'm?

DESIREE   Poking about in Tim Cantel's trunk.

ROSIE   We were not poking . . . Aiee! Whew! Just
                 shoving. Wooo . . . !

DESIREE   And I knew there was something fishy in here.
            It suddenly came to me.

            (ROSIE *ceases wringing.* ROSIE *and* DOCTOR
            look at her anxiously.)

ROSIE   Fishy?

DESIREE   (*pointing*) Yes – *that.* (DESIREE *bends down
            and picks up* MRS PRATT'S *distinctive looking
            cane. This has been lying on the floor,
            concealed from audience.* ROSIE *and* DOCTOR
            freeze.) What about that?

ROSIE   Ugh! Nasty looking thing! Whatever is it?

DESIREE   (*laughs*) What is it?

ROSIE   I've never seen anything like it before, have
            you, doctor?

DESIREE   Rosie! It's Mummy's cane!

ROSIE   Well I never! Relax, doctor, it's only Mrs
            Pratt's cane.

DESIREE   Well, what did you think it was?

ROSIE   Um – ah – a rather straight snake.

DESIREE   Mummy never goes anywhere without this cane.

ROSIE   She did this time.

DESIREE   Why?

ROSIE   Why? Well, she said 'I'm going to take a walk
            without my cane'.

DESIREE   Why?

ROSIE   I don't now why. Why does she do anything?

DESIREE   Unless she had someone near to give her a
            hand she never walked anywhere without it.

ROSIE   She had someone. The Squadron Leader.

DESIREE	Mummy ask Tim for help? Never.
ROSIE	I know why she left it behind. She said 'How am I going to get down those cellar steps carrying my cane? I'll trip over it and fracture my sk – ankle . . . ankle'. She said.
DESIREE	It all sounds most odd to me.
ROSIE	Well, you know what she was.
DESIREE	*Was?*
ROSIE	*Is!*
DESIREE	Well, I'd better bring her up. She could catch her death down there.
	(DESIREE *exits into hall, with cane.* ROSIE *sinks into the sofa, tears starting to flow.*)
ROSIE	I can't bear it.
DOCTOR	Now, Miss lake. There is plenty of time for guilty feelings later. Let us move this while we have the chance. You go to the top, much lighter.
	(ROSIE *and* DOCTOR *go each to one end of the trunk. They lift it and move it a couple of steps. It is clearly heavy.*)
ROSIE	You're going the wrong way.
	(MARK *enters from hall, carrying a raincoat.*)
MARK	Hi!
	(ROSIE *and* DOCTOR *drop trunk. It lands on* ROSIE'S *foot. She yells and does another Indian war dance.*)
ROSIE	Aieee . . . Owooo . . . Wooooo . . . Aah!
MARK	Let me guess. Indian war dance?

ROSIE   Yes.

MARK   Rosie Lake, you speak with forked tongue.
            What are you playing at?

ROSIE   Nothing. I thought you'd been arrested?

MARK   Arrested? Oh! You saw me leaving with that
            copper? No, he was going for his supper and I
            went for some fags.

ROSIE   You look very, very tired. Why don't you pop
            upstairs and have a nap?

MARK   I find taking naps just before going to bed a
            rather pointless exercise.

ROSIE   All the same, I don't like the look of you at all.
            Bed for you. I'll bring you up some Ovaltine.

MARK   I hate Ovaltine and don't offer me Horlicks
            instead because I hate that even more.

ROSIE   Hot milk? (MARK *shakes his head.*) Irish
            coffee? Rum and Coca Cola?

MARK   Why are you trying to get rid of me?

ROSIE   Whatever gave you that idea? Did you hear
            that, doctor? Ha, ha!

            (DOCTOR *and* ROSIE *both laugh hollowly, all
            too aware that* MARK'S *antennae are at full
            alert.*) Absolutely not! Why ever should we
            want to get rid of you?

MARK   Let's try another tack. What are you doing with
            Cantel's trunk?

DOCTOR/   (*together*) Nothing.
ROSIE   Moving it.

DOCTOR   Moving it.

MARK   Where?

Rosie	Why?
Mark	Why what?
Rosie	Why do you want to know where?
Mark	So I could help you hump it there, wherever where is.
Rosie	No! No! No! We're not moving it anywhere.
Mark	Just shoving it about for fun?
Rosie/ Doctor	(*together*) Yes! No!
Rosie	We were moving it back into the alcove.
Mark	Wasn't it already in the alcove?
Doctor/ Rosie	(*together*) Yes! No!
Rosie	Well, yes, *nearly*. We're pushing it further in because it was sticking *out*. Rather dangerous. The doctor shinned his bark on it.
Mark	Did he indeed? Lucky you're a doctor, doctor. Nasty business shinning your bark.
Doctor	Yes.
Rosie	No, he sharked his bin. Binned his shark.
Mark	As well? Better pop up to bed, doc, and Rosie will bring you some Ovaltine. She might even lace it with Coca Cola.
Doctor	I am quite well, thank you.
Mark	Relieved to hear it. There's a lot of shinning about. Ten new cases reported at Barking this week.
	(Mark *puts his raincoat down on trunk, then, still looking quizzically from one to the other,*

he prepares to sit on the trunk. ROSIE *lets out a cry.*)

ROSIE   Get up!

MARK   (*half rising again*) Why?

ROSIE   You mustn't sit down!

MARK   Why not?

ROSIE   (*losing her head*) You don't know where it's been.

MARK   My backside or the lid of the trunk?

ROSIE   Either. Both. Oh, take no notice of me.

MARK   I won't.

                (DESIREE *enters from hall, still carrying* MRS PRATT'S *cane.*)

DESIREE   She's not in the cellar.

ROSIE   Then she must have come up again.

DESIREE   No. Tim Cantel's down there pushing crates around and swearing.

ROSIE   He uses awful language. That's what drove your mother out of there.

DESIREE   He says she hasn't been down there and he hasn't seen her *at all*.

MARK   (*the cod policeman*) Now, now, what's all this then?

DESIREE   Mummy. She's disappeared.

                (MARK *rises, looking interested, no longer kidding.*)

MARK   How do you mean 'disappeared'?

DESIREE   Just that. She was here ten minutes ago. Now I can't find her anywhere.

MARK	What made you look in the cellar?
DESIREE	Rosie says she went down there with Tim.
MARK	(*to* ROSIE) Did she?
ROSIE	Well, I . . . think that's what she said. Yes.
MARK	But I thought they were at war.
DESIREE	Yes, but she and Rosie have some crazy notion that Mrs Privett-Smith may be buried there.
ROSIE	Ssssh! Desiree, please! (*To* MARK.) Just girls chat, you know. We didn't take it seriously.
MARK	Well! Who takes the odd body in a cellar seriously these days?
DESIREE	Something has happened to her, I know it.
	(DESIREE *looks ready to have a good cry.* MARK *puts a friendly arm round her shoulders, steers her towards hall door.*)
MARK	She'll be lurking around somewhere, probably waiting to pounce on Cantel. Come on, I'll help you look.
	(MARK *and* DESIREE *exit into hall.*)
ROSIE	I could kill that girl – FORGET I SAID THAT! (ROSIE *and* DOCTOR *move back towards the trunk.*) Poor Mrs Pratt. Isn't that strange? I could never get her name right and now she's gone I remember it perfectly. (*Near tears again.*) Bundling her into a trunk . . .
DOCTOR	You must not worry about Mrs Pratt. She is dead and gone.
ROSIE	She may be dead but she certainly isn't gone.
	(ROSIE *lifts* MARK'S *raincoat off the trunk to put it aside, This causes a piece of paper to*

fall from a pocket. She drapes raincoat over the back of a chair and picks up the paper.)

(*reacting.*) Doctor! Come here!

DOCTOR   Oh my goodness! We have no time . . .

ROSIE   This is important. (DOCTOR *moves to her.*) This is Mrs Privett-Smith's letter about Canada which Mark said he'd put down the loo.

DOCTOR   Yes!

ROSIE   So that was a pack of lies. He didn't destroy it. He *is* mixed up in this. I should go to the police if I could but I daren't. You can't report somebody for murder when you've just committed one yourself.

DOCTOR   (*anxiously*) Miss Lake, please let us get this trunk upstairs. After that we discuss other things.

ROSIE   Yes, you're right. (ROSIE *puts letter back in the raincoat pocket, then rejoins* DOCTOR *at the trunk. They lift it a little way out of the alcove. Shaken.*) Mark Anderson! And he seems such a nice boy.

DOCTOR   One, two three – lift.

CANTEL   (*offstage*) I don't know, I tell you!

(DOCTOR *and* ROSIE *drop the trunk. This time it lands and remains on one of* ROSIE'S *feet. Her face expresses exquisite agony.* CANTEL *enters.*)

What are you doing with my trunk?

ROSIE   Moving it back into the alcove. (*She gets her foot free.*) Aaaaah!

CANTEL   Who moved it out?

ROSIE   Um – Mrs Pratt was responsible.

CANTEL   She would be. There's no ruddy vodka in that
                  cellar, you know; nearly slipped a disc finding
                  out. I'm going down to the pub.

ROSIE   What a good idea! I'd never have thought of
                  that. Hurry, before it closes and don't hurry –
                  back, I mean.

                  (CANTEL *turns to exit but literally collides
                  with* DESIREE, *who enters with* MARK.)

DESIREE   (*to* CANTEL) You must have seen Mummy. If
                  Rosie says you and she were together . . .

CANTEL   Then Rosie must be telling the truth. Right?
                  Right! I confess, I hit her over the head, killed
                  her and shoved her in the trunk.

                  (ROSIE *utters a groaning cry and collapses
                  into a chair.*)

DESIREE   This is no time for jokes. A person can't just
                  vanish into thin air

CANTEL   You should be grateful if she has.

                  (CANTEL *makes as if to exit, changes his mind,
                  turns back to above his trunk. Watched in
                  horror by* ROSIE *and* DOCTOR *he kneels down
                  and flips open the clasp.*)

ROSIE   (*almost a shriek*) Stop! What are you doing?

                  (CANTEL *turns, at the same time fishing in his
                  pocket for a bunch of keys.*)

CANTEL   Just remembered it isn't locked.

                  (CANTEL *turns back and closes the clasp
                  again. lie now selects the appropriate key and
                  inserts it in the lock. This again is sheer
                  disaster time for* ROSIE.)

ROSIE   (*shrill*) Why are you locking it? You can't lock it.

CANTEL   Who says so?

ROSIE   I do! It isn't fair. It isn't necessary.

CANTEL   No? With old Daintee on the prowl things
           disappear and I've some silver cups in there.

ROSIE   I resent that, Squadron Leader.

CANTEL   (*completes locking*) You resent it, sweetheart,
           and I'll lock it. That way we'll both be happy.

           (CANTEL *pockets the keys and exits into hall.*)

ROSIE   Now him I could kill.

           (ROSIE *and* DOCTOR *whisper together.* MARK
           *joins them, startling them as they hiss at each
           other.*)

MARK   Can I help?

ROSIE   No.

DESIREE   I know! The attic!

MARK   What about the attic?

DESIREE   That's where Mummy may be if she wasn't in
           the cellar.

MARK   (*still playing detective*) Sounds logical.

DESIREE   (*severely, to* ROSIE) If anything's happened to
           her you're responsible. (ROSIE *makes a
           squeaking noise.*) Our doctor personally
           warned you what might happen if she overdid
           things. (*Moves to hall.*) Mark, would you take
           me upstairs?

MARK   Pardon?

DESIREE   To the attic. If Mummy's had one of her attacks
           she could be unconscious.

MARK   Lead on, Desiree. (*Aside to others.*) If we're not
           back in ten minutes, send out a rescue party.

(MARK *and* DESIREE *exit into hall.* ROSIE *and*
DOCTOR *are again left alone.*)

DOCTOR   (*peeking out of hall door*) Miss Lake, what did
              Mrs Pratt's doctor say to you? Did he tell you
              exactly what were these attacks of hers?

ROSIE   Yes, it was called something funny.
              Somebody's name. Like Smith's disease or
              Portnoy's complaint.

              (DOCTOR *moves from door, heads towards
              alcove.*)

DOCTOR   Hodgkins, Parkinson, Bright, Bell? A man's
              name?

ROSIE   I think so. One of those, I expect. I didn't really
              listen. I used to think she put it on.

DOCTOR   Coast is clear. Now we really can go.

ROSIE   (*hopelessly*) What's the use? He's locked her
              in. We can't get her out now, so why shift her?
              I'm done for,

DOCTOR   No. We may be able to force lock.

              (DOCTOR *faces towards the hall door and one
              end of trunk.* ROSIE *goes to the other end and
              has her back to the hall door.*)

ROSIE   I'll tell you one thing. If I get out of this I'll
              never commit another murder as long as I live.
              I'm not cut out for it.

              (ROSIE *and* DOCTOR *lift the trunk. They move a
              couple of paces out of the alcove.* JEAN SMITH,
              wearing a topcoat, enters from hall.)

JEAN   Good evening.

ROSIE   Aaaaagh!

(ROSIE *and* DOCTOR *drop the trunk. This time it lands on both her foot and his foot. They let out a joint chorus of pain.*)

DOCTOR/   (*together*) Oooh-eee aaaa-oww . . . Ooo!
ROSIE

(ROSIE *and* DOCTOR *extricate their feet.* ROSIE *manages a false sounding laugh and 'twists' briefly with* DOCTOR.)

ROSIE   Let's twist again. Oh, good evening. love.

JEAN   Have you seen Squadron Leader Cantel?

ROSIE   Yes. He went to the pub for a bottle of body . . . bodka . . . vodka.

JEAN   Then I'll wait for him here.

ROSIE   Will you? (*Angrily.*) What a silly place to wait.

DOCTOR   No! It is a good idea. (*To* JEAN.) You will excuse us. We are just taking his trunk upstairs.

JEAN   Let me help . . .

DOCTOR/   (*together*) No! No!
ROSIE

DOCTOR   No, thank you. It is very light.

ROSIE   Weighs nothing. (ROSIE *and* DOCTOR *lift the trunk again. Clearly it is not very light. Straining.*) It only *seems* heavy. Ha, ha!

(ROSIE *and* DOCTOR *start to move.* MARK *enters from hall.* ROSIE *and* DOCTOR *drop the trunk again.*)

MARK   The attic is clear. Not a body in sight. (*He sees* JEAN.) Hello. Rosie, do me a favour, will you?

ROSIE   That depends. What?

MARK	Push off for a minute. You too, doc.
ROSIE	I don't want to push off.
MARK	I have to whisper something to Miss Smith before the Squadron Leader returns to base.
ROSIE	You can go and whisper outside . . .
MARK	No, I can't. Shooo! (*Before* ROSIE *can gather herself* MARK *has pushed her out into the dining room. He stands aside for* DOCTOR *who also exits.* MARK *closes the door, turns to* JEAN, *shakes his head.*) I was rather hoping that you wouldn't come back.
JEAN	Of course, Mr Anderson, because you know who I am and why I'm here.
MARK	You credit me with fantastic powers of deduction. How would I know that?
	(JEAN *raises her handbag.*)
JEAN	For a start by snooping into this and finding out my real name and address.
MARK	(*nods*) Theoretically possible.
JEAN	At two o'clock this afternoon a man, who refused to give his name, telephoned my father, told him about Tim Cantel and me and suggested he call Scotland Yard to check up on Tim's criminal record.
MARK	Still rushing to conclusions, aren't you? Agreed, I could have looked into your bag, but how would I know about you and Cantel or that he has a criminal record?
JEAN	Either you're a detective or a crook.
MARK	(*smiles*) Did you decide which?
JEAN	Yes. A policeman wouldn't call anonymously. He'd say who he was.

MARK   Well, whoever or whatever the caller was, he did you a good turn, didn't he?

JEAN   I don't know. I don't know anything any more, but does he have to be condemned for the rest of his life because of a few past mistakes?

MARK   Could you describe his particular record a 'few past mistakes'?

JEAN   (*her voice breaking*) No. It was awful. Unbelievable.

MARK   (*gently*) Jean, go now. Don't bother to say goodbye.

                   (CANTEL *enters through hall door, carrying a bottle of vodka. He looks surprised to see* JEAN.)

CANTEL   Hullo! You're back early, Miss Smith.

MARK   If you two won't take it personally I shall leave you and pop into my bedroom slippers.

                   (MARK *retrieves his raincoat and exits into hall.* CANTEL *moves towards* JEAN *with open arms.*)

CANTEL   Missed you.

JEAN   (*moving back*) I want to talk, Tim.

CANTEL   So do I, but that doesn't . . .

                   (ROSIE *and* DOCTOR *enter from dining room. They are put out at the sight of* CANTEL *and he is irritated to see them.*)

ROSIE   Oh!

CANTEL   Damn!

ROSIE   Thank you *very* much.

CANTEL   Push off, Rosie, there's a love.

ROSIE

I will not push off. I've already been pushed off once.

CANTEL

Push off again.

ROSIE

Oh, all right and while you're doing whatever you're doing the doctor and I will take your trunk upstairs to get it out of the way.

CANTEL

No, you won't. I don't want it upstairs. I'm taking it away tonight. (DOCTOR *and* ROSIE *exit into hall, frustrated.*) Have you got your things all right, darling? We're leaving earlier than planned – like now.

JEAN

Why?

CANTEL

There's been a copper nosing around all afternoon asking questions about Mrs Privett-Smith.

JEAN

Who's she?

CANTEL

Old girl who lives here; disappeared with ten thousand nicker and all hell's broken loose.

JEAN

Why should that worry you?

CANTEL

It doesn't, but if she fails to show up, all kinds of questions will be asked – and that could lead to your father finding out about us.

JEAN

Tim, do you really have a job to go to in Bermuda?

CANTEL

Yes, I told you . . .

JEAN

I know you told me, but could you give me proof before we leave? (*A silence. She looks at him steadily. He looks away.*)

CANTEL

(*at last*) As a matter of fact, it's fallen through.

JEAN

Then you lied . . .

CANTEL

No. I only heard this afternoon.

JEAN	What did you plan to live on?
CANTEL	Well I've got the . . . a bit put by – enough to keep us going.
JEAN	Put by? From your salary at the flying club?
CANTEL	Well, I pulled off a couple of deals . . .
JEAN	Crooked? Thieving? That kind of deal?

(CANTEL *stiffens visibly. He has sensed trouble. Now he knows for sure.*)

CANTEL	Are you crazy? You don't really believe . . .
JEAN	That you could be a con man? Are you?
CANTEL	Just because I tell a white lie about the job you think I'm . . .
JEAN	Capable of depriving gullible old women of their life savings? Are you Tim?

(*Now* CANTEL *is completely silenced. It is clear she knows.*)

JEAN	(*inexorably*) How many times have you been to gaol? And why?
CANTEL	Who's been talking?
JEAN	Does it matter?
CANTEL	Of course it bloody matters! This is my life we're talking about.
JEAN	My father found out. He checked your record at Scotland Yard and read it to me this afternoon.
CANTEL	Christ . . . I . . . how awful! Look, I know how you must feel . . .
JEAN	Sick. Just sick.
CANTEL	(*despairingly*) But you came back.

JEAN

To say goodbye, that's all. (*A beat, her voice trembles*.) There is nothing more to say, is there?

CANTEL

Only that I love you. Can you forgive me?

JEAN

(*a shrug*) For what? You've done me no lasting harm. Can you forgive yourself? You have to live with you, Tim. I don't.

(*She starts to go.* CANTEL *makes a sudden move as if to embrace her, but* JEAN *exits hurriedly*.)

CANTEL

Jean, please.

(CANTEL *sits forlornly on chair by dining room door. He is thus hidden from hall door by the trunk.* ROSIE *crawls in on all fours from hall. She carries a screwdriver and a mallet. She crawls to left side of trunk and hits it.* CANTEL *gets on to all fours and crawls to right side of trunk.* ROSIE *hits trunk again. Both raise their heads above trunk and stare at each other for a moment. Then* ROSIE, *shattered by the sight of him, throws her black scarf over her face, turns on all fours and crawls out through* MARK'S *legs as he enters from the hall.* MARK *goes to the sideboard, picks up the now half empty whisky bottle and exchanges a knowing look with* CANTEL.)

MARK

I've just seen your Miss Smith. She seems upset about something.

CANTEL

I'm leaving here tonight, alone.

MARK

Not a lover's tiff?

CANTEL

More serious than that. Someone threw a spanner in the works.

MARK

Tough. I'm sorry.

CANTEL

You may have reason to be. Now there's nothing to stop me shopping you to the police.

MARK

What is stopping you?

CANTEL   Lucy Fordyce's piggy bank and any other cash
              you have stashed away upstairs, I want it.

MARK   I'll have to think about that one.

CANTEL   Don't think too long.

MARK   I've thought about it.

CANTEL   Then get it.

MARK   Stuff it.

CANTEL   You don't mean that. It takes one to know one.
              You're on the con, Anderson. You daren't take
              risks with the law.

MARK   (*indicating telephone*) Try me. 999, as usual.

              (DESIREE *enters from hall. She is in a highly
              nervous state but is doing her best to remain
              cool.*)

DESIREE   (*to* CANTEL) I've been right through the hotel
              from attic to cellar. I've been in every bedroom.

CANTEL   You raver, you.

DESIREE   (*accusingly*) Looking for Mummy. You saw her
              last. You took her to the cellar.

CANTEL   For the last time. I did not see her and I never
              went near the bloody cellar with her.

DESIREE   Yes you did. And I've told the police. (CANTEL
              reacts.) I phoned them from Rosie's office. I
              shall be waiting for them in the hall. So don't
              try to leave.

              (DESIREE *exits to hall.*)

MARK   I say, that hearty little worm is beginning to
              turn, isn't she? (CANTEL *does not reply. He is
              lost in some rather black thoughts.*) I'm still a
              bit puzzled at your lack of enthusiasm in
              reporting me to the police.

CANTEL	Simple. I don't give a damn what you've done. The money, any money, is more use to me then seeing you nicked for some piddling petty theft.
MARK	What a much better place the world would be if everyone was as broad minded as you!

(CANTEL *moves to telephone and puts a hand on it.*)

CANTEL	Do we have a deal?
MARK	I like playing poker, don't you?
CANTEL	Huh?
MARK	(*sits, folds his arms*) Which one of us is bluffing?

(CANTEL *hesitates, then lifts receiver and dials 999. He looks steadily at* MARK.)

CANTEL	(*phone*) Police, please. (*Pause.*) Police? Yes, I want to report a theft of a sum of money . . .
MARK	Hold it!

(CANTEL *stops talking, holds the receiver away from his mouth.* MARK *has risen and run to him.*)

CANTEL	(*to* MARK) You said something?
MARK	Hang up.

(CANTEL *smiles, hangs up.*)

CANTEL	Is that what they call poker?
MARK	I'd like a little time.
CANTEL	Half an hour and I want that money in my hot palm. (*Moves to door.*) You're out of your class, Anderson. Stick to Beggar My Neighbour or Snap.

(CANTEL *exits into hall.* MARK *looks thoughtful, moves to dining room door and exits. A brief pause. Hall door opens slowly and* ROSIE *puts her head in.*)

ROSIE   All clear.

(ROSIE *and* DOCTOR *enter.* ROSIE *carries a large bunch of assorted keys and also the hefty-looking screwdriver.*)

DOCTOR   (*nervous*) I still think it is better we do this upstairs.

ROSIE   How can we? The Squadron Leader's going up there now, isn't he? At least we can try these keys and if none of them fits we can fall back on the screwdriver. Keep cave outside the door.

DOCTOR   (*blank*) Keep . . . ?

ROSIE   Cave. Guard. If anyone comes bang on it loudly and sing out.

DOCTOR   Sing? Yes . . .

(DOCTOR *exits into hall, closing the door.* ROSIE *approaches the trunk, kneels down and starts to try various keys in the locks. She fails to get any one to turn. Finally she gets one stuck in which refuses to come out. In a panic she starts to tug at it.* MARK *enters silently from dining room. He starts to cross room, when he sees* ROSIE *who does not hear or see him.*)

ROSIE   Come on, you little b . . .

MARK   Rosie!

ROSIE   Aaaaagh!

(ROSIE *falls back and the key finally comes out. She regains her balance but turns to look at* MARK, *still on her knees.*)

MARK	Who do you think you are? Toulouse Lautrec? What are you doing rifling the Squadron Leader's trunk?
ROSIE	I wasn't.
MARK	Then why the hundred keys and a screwdriver?
ROSIE	I ... There was a screw loose . . .
MARK	You have a screw loose if you think that trunk is going to tell you anything. You already looked inside.
ROSIE	Absolutely! And not a body in sight – inside.
MARK	(*suddenly serious*) But you saw a body last night, Rosie, and somebody did crack you over the head. There was a murder here.
ROSIE	Now don't start that again after I'm perfectly happy thinking I'm barmy.
MARK	Rosie, I only have minutes to prevent a disaster. Think hard. Can you recall anything, anything at all, about the man who slugged you?

(ROSIE *opens her mouth to answer then clams it shut again.*)

ROSIE	Oh, no you don't! Remember? A knife in my back? Tim Cantel said it could be any one of you three. I don't see how it could be him. It certainly isn't the doctor but it was you lied about destroying that letter . . .
MARK	I'm a copper, Rosie.
ROSIE	And another thing . . . *Wha-at!* (MARK *briefly flashes an ID card and puts it back in his pocket.*) Then if the doctor didn't do it and you're a policeman . . .
MARK	(*nods*) Yes – Cantel. He has a prison record. His line is middle-aged ladies with a bit of money. He is also a murder suspect. Two of his

more recent ladies disappeared without trace. I
think Mrs Privett-Smith makes three.

ROSIE   But . . . but why bring her back here?

MARK   I don't think he did. I was tailing him on
             Saturday but, unfortunately, I lost him, so the
             rest is only guesswork. I think he met Mrs
             Privett-Smith who had the money with her. He
             planned to kill her then do a flit with a bird he's
             fallen for. (*Drily.*) He does have a human side.
             He'd forged and posted the letter about
             Canada. But something went wrong with the
             plan.

ROSIE   What?

MARK   (*shrugs*) Maybe Mrs P-S thought better of the
             whole thing. Maybe he turned out to be a lousy
             lover. Whatever it was, she decided to ditch
             him and come back here. Either he followed her
             or was waiting for her. He needs her money and
             he has to shut her mouth, so he kills her and
             then you came in.

ROSIE   Oh! And to think I rather fancied him myself! But
             wait! The body? What did he do with the body?

MARK   That's the jackpot question, Rosie. He must
             have had a brainwave.

ROSIE   He certainly would have had to. I was only
             unconscious for half a minute.

MARK   Something allowed him to kill her, slug you,
             hide the body and reappear only minutes later
             cool, calm, collected and confident no one
             would ever find it.

ROSIE   But there isn't anywhere. That policeman
             searched the place and now Desiree's been
             through it with a toothcomb looking for . . .
             (*Her eyes stray to the trunk and she falters.*)
             . . . and she didn't find any – body.

MARK   But it has to be here. Somewhere. In under five
            minutes he got the body out of this room, hid
            it, slipped out, got his trunk from the car and
            came back in.

ROSIE   It wasn't in the trunk?

MARK   No. If so, he'd have been safer leaving it
            outside on his car. Was there anything about
            his manner. anything he said which, in
            retrospect, gives us a clue?

ROSIE   No. The only strange thing that happened after
            he came in – and that had nothing to do with
            him – was the noise and thump I heard in Lucy
            Fordyce's room.

MARK   (*a bit impatient*) Forget the thump and stick
            with Cantel.

            (ROSIE *gives an audible gasp, drops the
            screwdriver, bends and picks it up, staring at
            it.*)

ROSIE   No! Let's stick with my thump.

MARK   Rosie . . .

ROSIE   Listen. Jean Smith just called me to her room –
            Lucy Fordyce's old room, because she couldn't
            make the gas fire work. There's a hole where
            the gas pipe goes into the floor near the tap.
            And in that hole I found this blocking the tap.
            It's not mine. I thought it might belong to the
            undertaker's men who'd used it to close the
            coffin.

MARK   Probably did.

ROSIE   Possibly did. I know what you all thought when
            I told you about someone moving in Lucy
            Fordyce's room and the thump, like something
            failing, But let's say I didn't imagine it, that I
            did hear movement, that I did hear something
            drop. What then?

MARK   It would mean that someone was in the room –
                but there wasn't, you said.

ROSIE   I didn't *see* anyone but then I didn't look
                behind the door and I didn't turn the light on.
                And there must have been someone there –
                him, the Squadron Leader.

MARK   Hiding the body in there?

                (*Triumphantly* ROSIE *waves the screwdriver at
                him.*)

ROSIE   Using *this!*

MARK   But . . . (*Suddenly gets it.*) Oh, my God! The
                coffin! Screwing the coffin down.

ROSIE   With not one but *two* little old ladies in it.
                There's his brainwave! You know, I *should*
                have been a detective.

MARK   You have to be right. Brilliant. Magic. He not
                only kills the lady, he makes her vanish in a
                cloud of smoke in Brighton Crematorium.

ROSIE   A pot of ashes – not a shred of evidence.

MARK   I'm afraid the bastard has got away with it.

ROSIE   I must have scared him when I opened that door.

MARK   Lucky you didn't walk in. You wouldn't be
                alive if you had.

                (*A loud knock from hall door. The* DOCTOR
                bursts in singing and gesticulating wildly.)

DOCTOR   (*singing*) 'Let's twist again like we did last
                Summer. Twist again . . .'

ROSIE   (*nerves gone*) What the hell do you think
                you're playing at?

(DESIREE *enters from the hall.*)

DESIREE   It really is disgraceful the time the police are taking to come. Rosie, can I make myself a cup of tea?

ROSIE   Go ahead, love. (DESIREE *exits into dining room.*) Doctor, didn't you say you wanted to come to my office to make a *trunk* call?

DOCTOR   No.

ROSIE   (*hissing*) Yes, you did.

(CANTEL *enters from hall.*)

CANTEL   Listen. Miss Daintee's doing a striptease on the landing.

ROSIE   Oh dear! That's something new and very nasty. Doctor, can you come and give her a junior aspirin.

(ROSIE *nods to* DOCTOR. *They both exit to hall.* MARK *and* CANTEL *are left alone.*)

MARK   Rather grim news, Flight Sergeant.

CANTEL   Oh? What's that?

MARK   The Brighton police just phoned through.

(CANTEL *goes very still but his face remains impassive.*)

CANTEL   When was this?

MARK   Couple of minutes ago. Luckily for you, I answered the phone. They stopped the cremation and opened up poor Fordy's coffin. You'll never guess what they found inside.

(*A beat.* CANTEL *looks at* MARK *steadily.*)

CANTEL   Two bodies. (*Laugh.*) Miss Fordyce and Mrs
              Privett-Smith.

MARK   Snap!

CANTEL   (*shakes his head*) Stick to snap and give up
              poker, son. You're a loser.

MARK   Novices have drawn four aces.

CANTEL   Not if another player already holds them.

MARK   You're that confident?

              (CANTEL *nods and grins. He is beginning to
              enjoy himself. Perhaps a little insanity begins
              to show.*)

CANTEL   Yes. The bell rings on my landing, too, and
              there's been no call since I got back. Naturally
              I've kept my ears open – just in case.

MARK   But I am right, aren't I?

CANTEL   (*nods, chuckles*) Bang on the nose. You must
              admit it was pretty good as a desperate piece
              of improvisation.

MARK   I'm lost in admiration.

CANTEL   She was scheduled to drop, suitably weighted,
              into the channel. Unfortunately, she went
              through my papers and found some rather
              unpleasant details about my past. Ran out on
              me just like that. She was obviously going to
              open her mouth . . .

MARK   So you closed it for her in here.

CANTEL   I intended to shove her in the trunk and take
              her away, then Rosie nearly gummed up the
              works. But suddenly it came to me. What could
              be more tidy than a nice double cremation?

MARK   No shame? No guilt?

CANTEL   I once went to a headshrinker. One thing he
          said always stuck in my mind – that the most
          useless emotion in this world is a guilty
          conscience. It never alters a thing. Well, I must
          love you and leave you.

          (CANTEL *lifts one end of the trunk and reacts in
          surprise to its weight.*)

CANTEL   What the hell . . . ? This bloody thing weighs a
          ton.

MARK   Don't ask me to help you. I'd be tempted to
          push you down the steps.

          (MARK *exits into hall.*)

          (CANTEL *produces key, unlocks the locks, flips
          up the clasp and opens the trunk.*)

CANTEL   God almighty!

          (*For the first time he is completely thrown, as
          he sees what the trunk contains.* DESIREE *enters
          from dining room carrying a cup of tea.*)

DESIREE   Oh! I just . . .

          (DESIREE, *too, can see inside the trunk and lets
          out a piercing scream, dropping the cup and
          saucer into trunk. In a panic,* CANTEL *leaps at
          her and tries to cover her mouth as she
          screams and screams again.*)

CANTEL   Stop that! Stop it!

          (DESIREE *fights fiercely and screams more.*
          ROSIE, *followed by* MARK *and* DOCTOR, *enter
          from the hall.*)

DESIREE   Mummy! Mummy! There! In the trunk!

          (ROSIE *and* DOCTOR *instinctively move together
          and clutch each other.* MARK *looks into the
          trunk. He feels down, probably touching one*

of MRS PRATT'S *hands.* DESIREE *flings herself at*
CANTEL, *flailing her arms.*)

DESIREE   You killed her! Killed her!

(MARK *drags her away.*)

MARK   (*to* DOCTOR) Take her upstairs, doc. Give her
something to make her sleep. (*Indicates trunk.*)
There's nothing we can do for Mrs Pratt, I'm
afraid.

(JEAN, *wearing pyjamas and a robe, enters
from hall, as* DOCTOR *leads* DESIREE *out.* JEAN
*gets a glimpse of the trunk and claps a hand
to her mouth to suppress a cry of horror. She
stares at* CANTEL *accusingly.*)

JEAN   Oh, no!

CANTEL   (*shrilly*) It wasn't me! Do you think I'm
completely crazy?

(*During ensuing lines* MARK *moves to trunk,
closes lid, drags it back into alcove and draws
the curtains to hide the trunk from view.*)

MARK   Probably, but fit to stand trial.

CANTEL   Never. This won't stick.

MARK   I don't know. You have a problem here, Timmy.
No handy coffin, no quicky cremation this time.

(*Front doorbell rings, off.*)

ROSIE   (*to* JEAN) Answer that, will you? I want to . . .
(JEAN *nods and exits to hall. To* MARK.) I think
I must tell you . . .

MARK   I don't know what you're going to say, Rosie,
but don't say it.

CANTEL   It's a plot, a bloody conspiracy.

MARK   (*gently*) That's right! Some naughty person
                with a grudge put her there. It doesn't matter
                that only you had the key and several of us
                heard you say you'd killed her and put her
                there.

CANTEL   I was joking, for Christ's sake! Do you think I'd
                have said a thing like that if I had killed her?

                (JEAN *enters from hall looks at* MARK.)

JEAN   It's a Police Inspector. He wants to . . .

                (CANTEL'S *nerve suddenly cracks. He runs to
                the window bay, parts the heavy curtains and
                runs straight into the bay. Almost immediately
                there is the crash of breaking glass as* CANTEL
                *evidently hurls himself right through the
                closed window.* MARK *makes no effort to
                pursue him, but runs out into hall.*)

MARK   (*yelling*) Get him! He went through the
                window . . .

                (ROSIE *heads towards the window, parts the
                curtains and looks out.* JEAN *exits into hall,
                looking after* MARK.)

ROSIE   He's broken my window!

                (*Offstage are heard voices, a police whistle
                and siren.* DOCTOR *enters from hall and
                approaches* ROSIE.)

DOCTOR   What is happening?

ROSIE   The Squadron Leader went berserk. He threw
                himself through the window. I'll put it on his
                bill.

DOCTOR   But why? He knows he did not do it.

ROSIE   Yes, but he doesn't know we know that he
                didn't do it. (*She heads to the sideboard and
                pours a hefty drink.*) Drink, doctor?

DOCTOR   (*promptly*) Yes, a large whisky please.

              (ROSIE *nods, does a delayed reaction, then pours him a drink.*)

ROSIE   How is Desiree?

DOCTOR   Lying down. By the way, she is not pregnant.

ROSIE   Thank goodness for that! (*Hands him a glass, raises hers.*) Cheers! Oh, what am I saying? I'll have to tell the police the truth, won't I? Whatever else he's done, I can't let him take the blame for this.

DOCTOR   (*unhappily*) I suppose.

ROSIE   I'll keep you right out of it, Doctor.

              (MARK, *followed by* JEAN, *enters from hall.*)

MARK   They caught him at the end of the road. He's not in very good shape.

ROSIE   I have to speak to you . . .

MARK   Just a sec. (*To* JEAN.) Jean, go to bed. The police won't need you tonight. (*Feels in pocket, produces a card which he hands to her.*) I may be away by the morning. Sometime, call that number and ask to speak to that fellow.

              (JEAN *looks at card, reacts in surprise.*)

JEAN   I don't understand. Who is he?

MARK   A well-intentioned heel. If he asks you out to dinner say 'yes'. (MARK *pushes her towards the hall door and places a gentle finger on her lips to prevent her saying more.* JEAN *exits.*) Good night. Try to get some sleep. You too, Doc.

DOCTOR   No, I must wait for police. However it may appear I think it possible Mrs Pratt is dying of natural causes . . .

MARK	(*pushing him to door*) Later. Go and watch the end of *Mummy's Coffin*. I believe it's terrific.
DOCTOR	(*resisting*) I have seen it twice and it is not in colour . . .
MARK	Don't let's bring race into this.
	(MARK *literally pushes* DOCTOR *from the room*.)
ROSIE	Mark, if you charge someone with murder, can you uncharge him if you've made a mistake?
MARK	Rosie, a few minutes ago I stood in this room and had to listen to Cantel confess to the murder of Mrs Privett-Smith.
ROSIE	He actually confessed? To *you*?
MARK	He doesn't know I'm a copper. I've fostered the impression that I'm another crook. He was risking nothing, anyway. Mrs Privett-Smith's ashes have been scattered over the South Downs . . .
ROSIE	(*stubbornly*) But I must talk about Mrs Pratt. I hit her . . .
MARK	(*cuts in*) I don't know how Mrs Pratt died and I don't want to know, but I do know that unless we pin her death on Cantel he'll go free, ready for his next murder. If ever there was a case of divine providence this is it.
ROSIE	You wouldn't have to live with it on your conscience.
MARK	Mrs Pratt is dead. Nothing can change that. And to be brutally frank she'll have done a lot more good in dying than she achieved in a lifetime of living, if we play it my way.
	(ROSIE *thinks, then in an almost symbolic gesture, she puts her glass firmly aside*.)

ROSIE   No, love. I'm sorry. I'll not see someone else
                 punished for what I did.

                 (*Front doorbell rings again.* MARK *makes a
                 helpless gesture.*)

MARK   That'll be the Inspector back.

ROSIE   Bring him in. I'll be waiting.

                 (*We may feel she is slightly enjoying the drama
                 of the occasion as she turns away and moves
                 towards alcove.*)

MARK   Oh Rosie! Why do you have to be so bloody
                 goodhearted?

                 (MARK *exits into hall.*)

ROSIE   There'll be no need for handcuffs. It is a far, far
                 better thing I do . . .

                 (ROSIE *opens the alcove curtains then, with
                 head averted, opens the lid of the trunk. With
                 a hint of martyrdom she turns her back to
                 alcove and faces the hall door. Then, with
                 what is hoped will be an even greater
                 theatrical effect, another jack-in-the-box
                 figure shoots up out of the trunk. It is* MRS
                 PRATT, *very much alive.* ROSIE *still faces the
                 door, quite unaware of what has happened.*)

MRS PRATT   What am I doing in this trunk?

                 (ROSIE *goes rigid, turns, points a trembling
                 finger, then her legs give and she sinks to the
                 floor in a dead faint.* MRS PRATT, *although
                 alive, is clearly not in top form. She ignores
                 ROSIE's condition. She steps out of the trunk
                 and stands swaying, supporting herself with
                 one hand on the open lid of the trunk.*)

MRS PRATT   I feel dizzy. I may be having one of my attacks.

                 (*The dizziness overcomes her and she sinks
                 into the nearest of the chairs. The curtain*

almost conceals her. DOCTOR *enters hurriedly from hall door.*)

DOCTOR   The police are . . . (DOCTOR *sees* ROSIE *lying on the ground and rushes towards her. He does not see* MRS PRATT.) Miss Lake! Miss Lake!

(DOCTOR *kneels down and half lifts* ROSIE *up.*)

MRS PRATT   Bring me a glass of water.

(MRS PRATT *stands up again, now in full view.*)

DOCTOR   Wait a moment, Mrs Pratt, I . . . (DOCTOR *suddenly freezes as he realises. He turns and looks at* MRS PRATT *and lets* ROSIE *drop to the floor with a loud thump. He utters an exclamation in his own tongue.*) Bhap re bhap!

MRS PRATT   Water!

(DOCTOR *suddenly claps a hand to his head and moves towards* MRS PRATT, *pointing a far from steady hand at her.*)

DOCTOR   The disease you have with the name of the man! (*Hits his own forehead angrily.*) Stokes Adams! You have Stokes Adams syndrome! (MRS PRATT *nods.*) The heart stops. No pulse. Seeming dead. Then the pulse starts again, but you can be unconscious . . . sometimes for hours . . .

MRS PRATT   I don't need your diagnosis, and don't send me a bill. I have my own physician. Get me a glass of water.

DOCTOR   Yes! Yes! Oh my God! You could have suffocated. We could have killed you. (DOCTOR *runs to sideboard, picks up water jug but finds it empty. He hurries with it towards dining room door.*) I am coming back. Sit, please sit. Take it easy. Oh my God!

(DOCTOR *exits into dining room.* MRS PRATT
*sinks back into the inglenook seat and is
again largely lost to view.* ROSIE *shows signs
of recovering her senses. She sits up on one
elbow and looks towards alcove. From her
position she would not see* MRS PRATT. MARK,
looking unusually excited, enters from hall.)

MARK   Rosie . . . ! (*Sees her.*) Rosie!

(MARK *kneels down and* ROSIE *clings to him.*)

ROSIE   I'll never drink again. Had the most dreadful
              hallucination; worse than pink elephants. I saw
              Mrs Pratt.

(MARK *has other matters on his mind.*)

MARK   Never mind about that. Listen. We're saved.
              The train taking the coffin to Brighton was
              hours late because of a derailment. The hearse
              which picked it up must have been driven too
              fast. It had an accident and they found her.
              They found Mrs Privett-Smith in Lucy's coffin.
              (MARK *does not see* MRS PRATT *rise to her feet
              again but* ROSIE *does. Her eyes bulge and she
              tries to speak, pointing a wildly wavering
              hand.*) Are you listening, Rosie? Cantel's had
              it – we've got him for the Privett-Smith murder.
              Mrs Pratt's death is immaterial.

(DESIREE *in an undesirable dressing-gown and
pyjamas, enters from hall.* DOCTOR, *with full
jug, enters from dining room.*)

MRS PRATT   (*thunderous, prodding* MARK *in the back*)
              Young man, will you please attend to me!

(MARK *turns, and sits flat on his backside,
staring at* MRS PRATT. ROSIE *passes out again.*
DESIREE *passes out cold near the hall door.*)

(*Blackout.*)

PROPERTY LIST

ACT ONE

Scene One

On sofa table:	*Radio Times, Knitting World* magazine (made up prop). Several other magazines, smal silver ornament.
On sofa:	Three cushions, open copy of magazine.
On telephone table:	Telephone, pad of paper, pencil.
On occasional table:	Silver ornament.
On sideboard:	Water jug with water, vase (empty), whisky bottle 1/3 full, glasses.
On floor behind high-backed chair:	Kukri knife (invisible).
On key rack:	Assorted keys.

Alcove curtains – closed.
Window curtains – closed.
Door to hall – open.
Door to dining room – closed.

Scene Two

CANTEL's trunk in alcove.
Both doors closed.
Alcove curtains – closed.
Window curtains – open.

Offstage

Opposite prompt side:
  Tray on which are four mugs, sugar bowl (empty) top hat with sugar in it.
  Small tray on which are an unbreakable cup and saucer.

Prompt side:
  Bunch of flowers in cellophane with card attached.
  Bottle of champagne.
  Gift card.

Biro (for CANTEL).
MISS DAINTEE'S bag.
Letter from Miss Privett-Smith.
Letter to DOCTOR.
Envelope containing money.
Full whisky bottle.
Urdu newspaper.
Full vodka bottle.
Trunk.
Dummy (dressed like MRS PRATT in Act Two).
Overnight bag (JEAN).
Magnifying glass.
Mallet.
Screwdriver.
Bunch of keys.

Personal properties:

ROSIE LAKE:	Coloured fan and scarf, black fan and scarf, black spectacles, jewelled spectacles, plainer spectacles.
MRS PRATT:	Cane, handbag containing smelling sales and handkerchief, black evening bag.
TIM CANTEL:	Bunch of keys, hotel bedroom key and front door key.
MARK ANDERSON:	ID card, visiting card, hotel bedroom key and front door key.
DOCTOR ALI:	Hotel front door key.
JEAN SMITH:	Handbag containing purse, money and diary.

Interval scene change:

Remove window frame from window.
Make up false window with masking tape.
Close curtains over window.
Remove champagne bottle.
Empty water jug.
Half empty new whisky bottle.
Tidy magazines.
Return silver ornaments to original positions.
Close both doors.

LIGHTING PLOT

Property fittings required:

> Three wall brackets.
> Two table lamps.
> Practical fire.

ACT ONE

Scene One – Night

To open: Virtual blackout except for glow from fire and small
            amount of night light through crack in closed
            curtains.

Cue 1:   Three wall bracket lights come on when THE LADY
            switches on at hall door. Not too bright effect as if
            room is only lit by wall brackets. (page 2.)

Cue 2:   Snap to original virtual blackout as GLOVED HAND
            switches off at dining room door. (page 2.)

Cue 3:   Snap on to same as Cue 1 as ROSIE switches on at
            hall door. (page 3.)

Cue 4:   Gloved Hand switches off lights again. (page 4.)

Cue 5:   Mrs Pratt switches on the lights. (page 5.)

Cue 6:   Snap to virtual blackout except for light from hall
            as ROSIE switches off at hall door. (page 10.)

Scene Two – Day

To open: Full daylight lighting state with daylight but *not*
            sun through windows. No cues.

ACT TWO

To open: Full lighting state with three wall brackets and
            both table lamps on. Good, bright artificial light
            effect. Fire is alight. No cues.

EFFECTS PLOT

ACT ONE

Scene One

Cue 1:   Two cats distantly miaowing. (page 2.)

Cue 2:   Two cats miaowing nearer. (page 2.)

Cue 3:   Two cats miaowing very loudly. (page 10.)

Scene Two

Cue 4:   MRS PRATT: "If you insist in using filthy language"
            – coffin bump. (page 23.)

Cue 5:   ROSIE: ". . . terrified they'll lock me up" – dinner
            gong. (page 37.)

Cue 6:   CANTEL: ". . . killed in the rush" – doorbell rings.
            (page 38.)

Cue 7:   MRS PRATT: ". . . remember your place" – telephone
            rings. (page 58.)

ACT TWO

Cue 8:   When MRS PRATT opens the door – voices off of
            ANDERSON and POLICEMAN. (page 67.)

Cue 9:   MARK: ". . . no quicky cremation this time" –
            doorbell rings (page 116.)

Cue 10:   As CANTEL leaps through window – glass crash.
            (page 117.)

Cue 11:   After glass crash – police whistle blowing and
            siren. (page 117.)

Cue 12:   ROSIE: ". . . punished for what I did" – doorbell
            rings. (page 120.)